GW00670526

Celebrating the Christian Year

Alan Griffiths is a priest of the Roman Catholic Diocese of Portsmouth. He studied Liturgy at the Pontifical Liturgical Academy of Sant' Anselmo in Rome and taught liturgical studies at Saint John's Seminary, Wonersh, from 1977 to 1983. He was a member of the panel that produced *Opening Prayers, Scripture-related Collects for Years A, B and C from the Sacramentary* (Canterbury Press, 1999) and has translated the Ambrosian Eucharistic Prefaces, published as *We Give You Thanks and Praise* (Canterbury Press, 1999). He has worked as a drafter and editor of texts for a National Proper collection commissioned by the Roman Catholic Bishops Conference of England and Wales. He works currently as a liturgical consultant active in the field of Church building and renovation.

Two further volumes in this series are in preparation.
Volume II: Lent, Holy Week and Easter
Volume III: Advent, Christmas and Epiphany
Both are due to be published in 2005.

Celebrating the Christian Year

Prayers and Resources for Sundays, Holy Days and Festivals – Years A, B and C
Volume I: Ordinary Time

Compiled by Alan Griffiths

First published in 2004 by the Canterbury Press Norwich
(a publishing imprint of Hymns Ancient & Modern Limited,
a registered charity)
St Mary's Works, St Mary's Plain,
Norwich, Norfolk, NR3 3BH

www.scm-canterburypress.co.uk

British Library Cataloguing in Publication data

A catalogue record for this book is available
from the British Library

ISBN 1-85311-568-1

Typeset by Regent Typesetting
Printed and bound by
Biddles Ltd, www.biddles.co.uk

CONTENTS

INTRODUCTION

This book contains a selection of prayer text resources for the Eucharist or Main Service on the Sundays and significant holy days that fall between Epiphany and Lent and between Pentecost and Advent. It also contains some material for other types of service.

I hope that this book will be useful to those Anglican parishes and communities that use the Lectionary of *Common Worship* for their main service. However, I intend that it will have a broader appeal. I hope that it will be equally useful for all those who use lectionaries based either on the Roman Catholic Sunday Lectionary or on the *Revised Common Lectionary*.

It is one of the great ecumenical advances of recent years that the 'mainstream' churches (and others too) are now using a pattern of readings for Sunday services that has a common thread running across the denominations. The significance of this lies in a common conviction that the riches of the Scriptures ought to be more widely available to the Church's worship. This in turn rests on a common conviction that it is the Word of God that both calls us to worship and shapes our response to that call.

I hope that this fact will extend the interest of this book beyond the Church of England and make it useful to all who desire to worship in something resembling a modern English vernacular.

The Sunday Lectionary contained in *Common Worship* is based on the Three Year Cycle of the *Revised Common Lectionary*, itself inspired by the *Ordo Lectionum Missae* (Order of Readings for Mass), created after the Second Vatican Council for the Liturgy of the Roman Catholic Church.

The basic insight of this lectionary was that the Gospels and other documents of the New Testament should be allowed to speak to the Church in a form as uninfluenced as possible by choices of theme or subject. The reading of the Synoptics was planned so that on the 'Ordinary Time' Sundays of the Church's Year (corresponding to the Sundays covered in this book) each Gospel should be read through in order over a three-year period, with Saint Matthew in Year A, Saint Mark in Year B and Saint Luke in Year C. The Gospel of Saint John is read in its entirety each year. The Letters of the New Testament are treated in a similar manner.

The Roman Lectionary system was refined and augmented in the *Revised Common Lectionary*, and later still by the *Common Worship* Lectionary, which allowed a greater role for the Hebrew Scriptures and some other differences to both its predecessors.

In the *Common Worship* Lectionary and Calendar, the Sundays after Epiphany form an extended celebration of the Epiphany/ Baptism of Christ lasting until the Feast of the Presentation of Christ in the Temple, known popularly as Candlemas, followed by a pre-Lent season. Then, after Pentecost and before All Saints' Day, there follows a series of Sundays when there is no particular festal focus. Lastly, between All Saints' and Advent, the Sunday readings reflect a more 'eschatological' theme suitable for the falling of the year and the coming of the Feast of Christ the King and the Season of Advent. This is known in some quarters as the 'Kingdom Season'.

The idea of providing additional resources to those given in the 'official' service books of the Church of England is not new. A collection of texts for Saints' days to supplement the provision in *The Alternative Service Book*, entitled *The Cloud of Witnesses* (Alcuin/Collins 1982), was soon followed by the series of three volumes entitled *Lent, Holy Week and Easter* (Church House/ SPCK 1984), *The Promise of His Glory* (Church House/ Mowbray 1991) and *Enriching the Christian Year* (SPCK/Alcuin 1993). *Patterns for Worship* (Church House 1995) followed soon after. The coming of *Common Worship* has been followed closely by *New Patterns for Worship* (Church House 2002). A much larger collection of liturgical prayers, partly in book form, partly on disk, is forthcoming.

The provision of liturgical resources to meet all kinds of needs might be described as a growth industry these days. It reflects the need that parishes and other communities experience to seek and evolve liturgical forms that suit them, as well as expressing the worship of the Church as a whole. This need has to be accompanied, though, by the willingness of churches to understand themselves, make informed choices and plan their worship with due care.

This volume is centred on a particular idea, that of allowing the scriptures spoken at worship to influence aspects of the prayer of the congregation and those who lead them. A set of prayers has therefore been created which takes inspiration from the themes and imagery of the Scripture readings proclaimed on Sundays and feast days.

This idea came originally from the publication of *Opening Prayers*, subtitled *The ICEL Collects* (Canterbury Press 1999). These texts were prepared originally by The International Commission for English in the Liturgy, a commission set up by English-speaking Catholic bishops immediately after the Second Vatican Council to translate for liturgical use the newly revised liturgical books of the Roman Catholic Church. The preparation of the collects formed part of the programme of producing a second edition of the 1973 ICEL translation of the Roman Missal.

New, Scripture-related, prayers had been requested by the English-speaking bishops and others during a consultation held prior to the initiation of the project during the 1980s. Accordingly, the 'ICEL Collects', created in the years between 1986 and 1993, originated as a collection of prayers intended for Roman Catholic use as alternatives to the Collect at Mass, and based on the Scripture readings for the day.

I decided, therefore, that a similar collection of Scripture-related collects based on the *Common Worship* Sunday and Festal Main Service Lectionary might be appropriate. I have already drawn attention to the fact that though this Lectionary follows much of the Roman/Revised Common Lectionary pattern, it deviates from it significantly enough at certain times of the year to suggest a need for a new collection of Scripture-based prayers. This is what I am attempting to provide.

As far as I am aware, those responsible for the *Common Worship* family of texts have chosen not to prepare Scripture-related prayers for the Sundays and feasts of its Lectionary. This is due partly to the view of the Church of England Liturgical Commission that the function of the Collect is to provide a moment of prayer designed to conclude the opening moments of the service.

While I respect this approach, I do not necessarily agree with it. It seems to me that in practice the role of the Collect is more sophisticated. The Collect seems to serve two functions, like a bridge, closing the 'entrance rites' but also initiating the Ministry of the Word. Therefore a prayer that is recognizably related to the readings that will follow it, while not being so closely bound up with them as to be unavailable for use at other times, seems to be desirable. The success of *The ICEL Collects* appears to bear out this view.

Since the Scripture readings for the Propers 4–21 have a two-track approach, one opting for a continuous reading of significant parts of the Old Testament over three years and the other for a choice of Old Testament reading that reflects the Gospel selection, I have also attempted to provide collects to accompany those who opt for this 'continuous reading' track. I have not succeeded in finding appropriate material for each Sunday, but the provision reflects the shape and course of the narrative as a whole, and the same prayer might, if desired, be repeated over two or more Sundays.

In addition to the newly created texts of the Scripture-related prayers, I have provided other material for use at other parts of the Service. A note on sources appears at the end of this Introduction, page xix.

The Role of Sunday

It might seem unnecessary to write about the significance of Sunday in a collection of liturgical texts. All Christians know that Sunday is special. However, in our society it is no longer clear that Sunday is a unique day for Christians, or why that should be. Many Christians themselves seem confused as to what Sunday really is all about. So perhaps some restatement of what makes Sunday the primary feast day of Christians might be appropriate.

The root of this matter is to be found in two factors. First, believers live in what might be described as a symbolic universe. It is, as it were, a virtual place, civilization or culture, determined, expressed and maintained by a symbolic language. Dogma, worship and spirituality, a particular attitude to the world, issues, neighbour and so on, are all part of that symbolic culture, which is, of course, expressed by Christians who exist within the 'other' culture, that of empirical science and technology – and the need to get on with life – in which we all live.

Secondly, a characteristic of that symbolic universe is its enactment of time. Judaism, Christianity and Islam live within the temporal symbol of a sacred week with a sacred day at its heart. This contrasts with that other symbolic calendar which most people use to determine their 'religious' practice, if any. This calendar, in origin a pagan one, is based not on the sacred week but on the sacredness of certain occasions within the annual or the life cycle, such as birth, marriage and death, occasions when most people 'go to church'.

For Christians, the sacred or symbolic week centres on Sunday as its beginning. Christians made the change from the Jewish Sabbath very early on, within the New Testament period in fact. It might be argued that this revolutionary change stands as a witness to the reality of the Resurrection of Jesus, since little else could explain such a radical change of religious usage. The first Christians coined the title 'The Lord's Day' for Sunday. 'The Lord' – the Jewish title for God – is now applied to Christ, the risen One. We know that the observance of Sunday predates the observance of any other feast, even (probably) Easter itself. Sunday, then, is the day of Christ's rising, the day of his 'passover' from death to life.

In ancient and traditional Christianity, Sunday is presented as 'The First Day'. It is the Day of Creation, part of a narrative reconstructed by Christians as a foreshadowing of the new creation inaugurated in the risen Lord. It is this connection with the dying and rising of Christ that makes Sunday the traditional day for the celebration of Christian baptism, the first of all the sacraments.

Sunday is also the day of the Eucharist, 'The Lord's Service on the Lord's Day' as the movers of the Parish Communion Movement in the Church of England used to say last century. Inasmuch as Christian tradition understands the Eucharist as a memorial enactment of the whole event of Christ's dying and rising, perpetual intercession and return in glory, then its connection with Sunday is clear. The dynamism and power of the Eucharist is the presence of the risen Christ, in the Holy Spirit.

If Sunday is the Day of the Lord and of the Eucharist, then it is also the Day of the Church. For the Church is constituted by the proclaimed Word of God and the eucharistic Table of Christ, which together form a complete act of worship. The Eucharist makes the Church, even as the Church 'does' the Eucharist.

Sunday has also been seen as the 'Eighth Day', the day that stands outside the seven created days as the last, the uncreated, the greatest and the everlasting day. Its sunrise is the resurrection of Jesus, and it will have no sunset. One of the prefaces for 'The Lord's Day' (cf. p. 127) tells this story.

So Sunday is not 'The Sabbath'. Despite generations of usage of that title, it is simply mistaken. Christians have transferred Jewish observance – rest and celebration – to Sunday, but to call it the 'Sabbath' is incorrect. This is especially obvious when one looks at many oriental Christian traditions that, though centred on Sunday, still keep Saturday as a special day, an echo of its Jewish significance.

The observance of Sunday functions as the 'skeleton' or 'deep structure' of the Christian symbolic year. The great seasons are all 'Sundays before' or 'Sundays of' or 'Sundays after' something.

The Content of this Book

In this book, I have collected special texts for each Sunday and feast day as follows:

- A **Scripture-related opening prayer:** that is a collect for each of the years A, B and C created on the basis of the Scripture readings of the day. The rationale for these has been set out already.
- An alternative collect or **opening prayer.** This offers a further choice to those who do not wish to use the *Common Worship* collect at this point. I have tried as a whole (though not always successfully) to keep the style of this prayer somewhat simpler than that of the Scripture-related opening prayer.
- A verse to be sung with the **Acclamation** *Alleluia* before the Gospel reading. The shout 'Alleluia' – 'Praise God!' – though new at this point to many Anglicans, is traditional before the Gospel, as a greeting to the procession with the book of Scripture containing the Gospel reading. The verse should always be used with 'Alleluia' as its refrain. The traditional way of doing this with cantor or choir is set out in each section of this book. If a procession is going to be a long one, then a hymn might be sung before the Alleluia and verse. There is precedent for this in the many medieval poems or 'sequences' that were used as songs before the Gospel.
- A collect which may be used to conclude the **Intercession.** This third collect is often cast as a prayer on behalf of the Church as a whole, or with a 'Church' theme, which makes it suitable for use at this point.
- A **Prayer over the Gifts,** which may be used after the preparation of the Eucharistic Table and before the Eucharistic Prayer. The idea for a prayer at this point in the Rite originates in the Roman Church. In the Roman tradition this short collect usually speaks of the gifts being 'offered' at the altar, although the understanding is that the Eucharistic Prayer itself articulates this aspect of the Eucharist. Many Anglicans,

inheriting the traditional Reformed suspicion of 'offering' language at this point, would not find most of the Roman prayers acceptable. I have therefore proposed prayers that refer either to the Eucharistic Prayer itself, asking for the words to praise and thank God, or to the fellowship of the Lord's Table, initiated by the Eucharistic Prayer and Communion. These seem to be the aspects that it is most important to refer to at the 'taking' of the Bread and Cup.

- A **Eucharistic Preface** for each of the Sundays of Epiphany and between All Saints' and Advent, which may, if appropriate, be used as the opening of the Eucharistic Prayer. A small selection of prefaces for the Sundays between Pentecost and All Saints has also been included. Most of the prefaces are taken from *We Give You Thanks and Praise, the Eucharistic Prefaces of the Ambrosian Rite* (Canterbury Press 1999).
- A **Prayer after Communion**. This collect should be used directly after the administration of Holy Communion. Like the collect at the beginning of the service and the prayer at the preparation of the table, it also has a double reference. It looks back to the eucharistic meal, and forwards, either to the mission of the Church which is enacted and inaugurated by the Eucharist, or to the eschatological 'Supper of the Lamb' of which the Eucharist is the foretaste and pledge.

For the festivals, a similar selection is offered, except that there is only one Scripture-related opening prayer in each case, since there is only one set of readings.

The Sunday and festival Main Service provision occupies the bulk of this book. However, I have attempted also to suggest material that might form part of services to prepare for the great festivals, Candlemas and All Saints', that mark turning points in the Calendar, as well as forms for a community commemoration of the dead and a special service for the sick, including the laying on of hands and anointing if desired. There are also some texts for rites to begin a solemn celebration of Saturday Evening Prayer or Sunday Vigil service.

Details

The Conclusion of Collects

Collects usually end with an acknowledgement that prayer is made to the Father through Jesus Christ. The traditional ending is *Through Jesus Christ our Lord*, Response: *Amen*. For a more 'solemn' ending, often employed with the opening Collect, the Trinitarian relationships are invoked in something like this form:

Through Jesus Christ (your Son,) our Lord
who is alive, and reigns with you
in the unity of the Holy Spirit,
one God, for ever and ever.

These endings may be used with most of the collects in this book. However, I have tried to vary the ending, partly to allow for those who have difficulty with words like 'Lord' and 'reigns' (and might prefer the simple 'Through Jesus Christ: Amen.') and partly to allow for variety. Those preferring to use the more traditional endings may substitute them for the ones given in the body of the text.

The Beginning and Ending of the Prefaces

Traditionally, the first line of the Preface echoes the congregational response: 'It is right to give thanks and praise' – 'It is truly right . . .' However, this is not always the case. In *Common Worship* other openings are proposed, particularly in the extended prefaces.

I have usually kept to the traditional opening for the Preface in this book. However, there are variants on it. The one most often used resembles the traditional 'echo' opening by echoing an earlier line of the dialogue between president and congregation: 'Lift up your hearts', and begins something like this:

We lift up our hearts to you,
God eternal, true and faithful;

to you we offer thanks and praise
through Jesus Christ your Son.

Preface openings are usually interchangeable, so if this form is preferred, it can be used with most of the prefaces in this book.

The Preface ending also varies. The traditional ending names the various ranks of heavenly beings, angels, archangels, thrones, dominions, powers and so on. However, there are other, shorter, forms, such as:

And so, with angels and saints,
we glorify your holy name:

Again, these Preface endings are usually interchangeable. The dynamic of the liturgy demands, however, that the congregation is cued to enter with 'Holy, Holy . . .'

Last Word

The Style of the Collect Form

The question of how to articulate prayer, what sort of language to use, how much 'literary' influence there should be, is one on which opinions are legion. Since the era of liturgical reconstruction began about forty years ago, the debate has become more lively.

The Church of England has opted for an approach that allows both for formal style (the collects in *Common Worship*) and a more informal address (such as the simpler collects in *New Patterns for Worship*), and indeed for just about everything in between. Given the need for choice, this is surely wise.

The form of a collect as we have it originated probably in the Roman Church, famed for its terse and economical prose style. Other ancient Latin churches also employed it, alongside more lengthy styles of prayer.

The collect form was probably devised at the same time as the liturgy of the Church of Rome changed from largely Greek to largely Latin, some time in the fourth century CE. It is a carefully contrived literary artefact consisting of address, narrative, petition and conclusion. The narrative element is nearly always a relative clause. This serves to heighten the force of the petition, and allows the whole prayer to exist as one single sentence or period. It is important to understand this internal dynamic of the 'collect form', as it represents much more than a literary feature.

The 'movement' of the collect is deeply rooted in the dynamic of biblical prayer and confession of God's name. The prayers of the Bible allow for the remembrance of God's mighty works in the past to serve as the basis for petition for God's work in the future. The psalms and canticles of the Hebrew Scriptures are the best illustrations of this dynamic. It is, too, the overall dynamic of the Eucharistic Prayer, which moves from past to present and to future, where the final 'Amen' becomes eschatological.

The Roman collect was brilliantly converted into a thoroughly English prayer form by Thomas Cranmer in the sixteenth century for the *Book of Common Prayer*. Both as translator and as author, Cranmer retained the terseness and elegant economy of the Roman collect, while adjusting its syntax to serve his native language with its different grammatical and rhetorical traditions. We owe him a tremendous debt.

More recently, ICEL and others have made attempts to bring the collect form up to date. The result was often the suppression of the relative clause and its replacement by a direct statement in apposition to the address. This gave us the 'Almighty God, you sent your Son . . .' form. The reason given for this adaptation is that the old second person singular 'thou' and its associated verbal forms are no longer employed in English, so 'Almighty God, who gavest thy Son . . .' would have to be literally rendered as 'Almighty God, who gave . . .' This is all right when the syntax is simple, but more difficult to render successfully when it is complex. Those who do not like the 'You gave' form maintain it loosens the structure of the collect and, in effect, tells God as direct statement what God already knows.

My judgement is that in practice (if not in Academe) we can afford to loosen the structure, and indeed that in enumerating the character and qualifications of someone we habitually use the 'You did this/that' form and not the relative clause. I do not see how this is any more 'telling God what God already knows' than is the 'O God, who gavest' form. However, I would retain the relative clause wherever possible, simply because in its simplest forms it sounds well and offers no impediment to understanding on hearing.

The prayers in this book all reflect this composite view of the contemporary collect. It seems that the sources all find it possible to use both relative and direct address forms in various ways. The collects (largely the Scripture-related opening prayers) created specifically for this book use both methods.

Reverence or Informality?

How 'formal' should liturgical language be? The current debate, at least in some quarters, is becoming increasingly polarized and seems to be increasingly a dialogue of the deaf. This is a pity, since the question, albeit a very general one, can be approached intelligently.

The answer needs to be thought out in terms of what liturgical language is for. In human terms, liturgical prayer is an attempt to articulate the many thoughts, intentions and acts of devotion of a diverse community. It has, therefore, the primary need to be heard clearly by everyone, as it should be part of a dialogue that is mouth to ear and ear to mouth, a dialogue where the printed text has a lesser place.

Furthermore, it should have a certain predictable formality, to allow everyone to know where they fit into it, if only to know when to say 'Amen.' Traditional prayers are creative within a well-known template. If this is 'formality' then its employment is a pastoral necessity, a clear benefit to all. Extempore prayer tends to squeeze out any real engagement by the congregation, rendering them listeners rather than participants and, it must be said, subjecting them unnecessarily to the whims and possible manipulations of the speaker. So a degree of formality is essential in common prayer.

Liturgical language needs also to reflect our approach to the apparent paradox of God's utter transcendence and utterly transcendent immanence. We believe in one God, 'high and lofty', but One who has revealed Godself as Trinity, a communion, intimate exchange.

So the difficulty is always the fine line to tread between a breezy confidence that seems to want to tell God what God should be doing and an affectation of reverence, which will have no resonance with vernacular speech and will sound like a cringing before God.

The Lord's Prayer, which is a supreme act of collaborative submission to God, yet begins with Jesus' preferred mode of address: 'Our Father'. The Latin introduction '*Audemus dicere*' is rightly translated by 'We dare to say . . .' So words expressing the majesty of God and the modesty of the petitioners are proper to prayer: 'We pray/ask/seek/beg'. But then so is the more tender and intimate language of some of the Psalms:

Whom have I in heaven but you?
And there is nothing upon earth that I desire
in comparison with you. (Psalm 73:25)

You encompass me behind and before
and lay your hand upon me. (Psalm 139:4)

As it is a compendium of diverse sources, all I can hope for is that I have managed to encompass these many legitimate differences of style in this book.

The Sources of this Collection

The sources used for this collection include many that are not from the Anglican tradition, since other available collections of liturgical resources draw heavily on the prayer books of other parts of the Anglican Communion. A full note on sources can be found in the 'Sources and Acknowledgements' section at the end of the book. However, I thought that a word of introduction might be appropriate.

The Scripture-related opening prayers, one for each of the three years of the cycle of the lectionary, have largely been created by myself, with help from friends.

A major source for other texts has been the Third Typical Edition of the Roman Missal, published in 2002. The Missal contains a huge collection of prayers (some 1600 collects alone), many of which are also suitable for Anglican use. The translation of these prayers has been my own. I have employed criteria for translation similar to those adopted by ICEL in its 1998 translation of the Missal. I have made some amendments that will allow these prayers to be appropriate for use in Anglican and other communities. I have tried to keep a doctrinal consistency between the Roman material and the doctrine embodied in the prayers of *Common Worship*.

Lastly, a word about the Ambrosian Liturgy, from which most of the prefaces and some of the other prayers are derived. Readers unfamiliar with this tradition may be interested to learn that the Church of the Diocese of Milan has for hundreds of years had its own characteristic forms of worship for the Mass and Daily Prayer. The tradition in the diocese traces the origins of these forms back to Saint Ambrose, Bishop of Milan from 374–397 CE. After the Second Vatican Council, the diocese revised its liturgy, and the distinctive Ambrosian forms have now acquired a new vitality in a very active diocese.

The presence of a liturgical tradition differing from that of Rome is unusual in the Roman Catholic Church, where the Roman Liturgy has, over many centuries, come to predominate and other local liturgies, such as the so-called 'Mozarabic' Liturgy in Spain and the ancient Latin Liturgies of Gaul, have, until recently, all but disappeared.

Alan Griffiths
24 June 2003
The Birth of Saint John the Baptist

PART ONE

PROPER TEXTS FOR THE SUNDAYS AND MAJOR FEASTS BETWEEN EPIPHANY AND LENT

Between Epiphany and the Festival of the Presentation of Christ in the Temple, popularly known as Candlemas, the Lectionary and service texts form an extension of the celebration of Christmas/Epiphany.

The precedent for this is in the old lectionaries, which prolonged the Epiphany season in a commemoration of the Baptism of Jesus and first sign that he gave in Cana of Galilee. It seems that the custom of concluding the celebration of the Christmas/Epiphany events with the celebration of the Presentation on 2 February may also be of some antiquity. The prayers and prefaces suggested in this section reflect this. It is of interest to know that the Ambrosian Liturgy in Milan continues this tradition with the 'Epiphany' tone of its first three prefaces for the Sundays and weekdays of Ordinary Time, which will naturally fall in January. These texts are set out below.

Because of the variable date of Easter, the number of Sundays between Candlemas and Lent is not fixed. However, themes traditional to this time (the weeks and Sundays formerly known as Septuagesima, Sexagesima and Quinquagesima), such as the opening chapters of the Book of Genesis, are retained in the lectionary of *Common Worship*.

The Sunday after Epiphany (First Sunday of Epiphany) is celebrated as the festival of the Baptism of Christ.

The Baptism of Christ
The First Sunday of Epiphany

The Eastern churches celebrate the Baptism of Christ at Epiphany, as the manifestation ('epiphany' in Greek) of the Son of God. In the early Middle Ages, those Latin-speaking churches liturgically independent of the Roman Church seem to have done the same. In the eighth century, the churches influenced by the Roman Liturgy (which celebrated Epiphany mainly as a commemoration of the visit and homage of the Magi) began to commemorate the Baptism of the Lord during the days following Epiphany. The feast became part of the Sunday cycle of the Roman Catholic Church in 1960, and The Alternative Service Book *fixed it on the Sunday after Epiphany in 1980.*

Scripture-related opening prayers

Year A
All-holy God,
whose beloved Son desired to receive
the baptism of repentance to fulfil all righteousness;
grant that, as he chose to become one with sinners,
so we, being made one with him in baptism,
may accept his justice
as the very truth of our life;
for Christ is our Lord, now and for ever.

Year B
At the beginning of creation, O God,
your Spirit swept over the waters,
and at the baptism of Jesus, your Son,
that same Spirit came down
to anoint him as the Christ.
Grant that all your baptized people
may recognize their Christian dignity
and so live as to be found worthy of it.
We ask this through Jesus Christ,

who is one with you and the Holy Spirit,
for ever and ever.

Year C
God of glory,
in the baptism of your beloved Son
you revealed the anointing of the Spirit
and foretold the baptism that is to come.
Let us not fear the closeness of your judgement
but rather, by good and faithful discipleship,
let us prepare on earth the foundations
of your heavenly kingdom,
so that when, on that last day,
your voice will shake the universe,
we may stand with joy to welcome
the One who is to come and bless us with peace;
Jesus Christ, whose reign is for ever and ever.

Opening prayer

Years ABC
Gracious God,
through the Holy Spirit
you have revealed to us
the Beloved One, your child and servant,
into whose death we are baptized.
Keep us faithful
as witnesses to his resurrection,
for he is alive, and glorious for ever and ever.

Acclamation

Years ABC
V/. Alleluia, Alleluia, Alleluia.
R/. Alleluia, Alleluia, Alleluia.
V/. The heavens were opened and the voice of the Father was heard:

'This is my Son, the Beloved; the One on whom my favour rests.'
R/. Alleluia, Alleluia, Alleluia.

Intercession

Years ABC
Holy God,
let your abundant blessing
descend from heaven upon your Church,
to confirm and create anew
those who in the sacrament of baptism
have been washed in water
and born again in the life-giving Spirit.
We ask this through Jesus Christ our Lord.

Prayer over the Gifts

Years ABC
With bread and wine,
with praise and thanksgiving, O God,
we come to the table you prepare
for your baptized people.
Through your Holy Spirit,
let us enter here into the fellowship of Christ,
and into the movement of his self-offering,
for he is alive for ever and ever.

Eucharistic Preface

Years ABC
It is truly right and just, our duty and our salvation,
always and everywhere to give you thanks,
Lord, holy Father, almighty and eternal God.

In the voice from heaven over the Jordan river
you revealed yourself as the Saviour of all

and the Father of the eternal Light.
You rent the heavens, blessed the air
and purified the springs of water;
then by the Holy Spirit in form of a dove descending
you announced the advent of your Only-Begotten Son.
Today the waters received your blessing,
to wash away our ancient curse,
to grant believers the forgiveness of sins
and make them your very own children
by a heavenly birth into eternal life.

And so, with all creation on this joyful feast,
we acclaim you, the source of life and goodness,
in this holy and exultant song: Holy . . .

Prayer after Communion

Years ABC
Lord, in the strength of this food from heaven
let us walk as children of your light,
and be your beloved sons and daughters
both in title and in truth.
We ask this through Christ our Lord.

The Second Sunday of Epiphany

Scripture-related opening prayers

Year A
You are glorified, O God
in the One you have declared
to be your servant and your Son.
Be glorified also in those he has called
to be disciples and saints.
Keep fresh in them the baptism they have received
and let the Creator Spirit

daily renew and fashion their lives
into a joyful announcement of your good news.
We ask this through Jesus Christ our Lord.

Year B
God of wonderful knowledge,
whose voice calls each of us by name;
you confound our expectation
by revealing yourself to the lowly.
Confound also our fear,
that we may not be afraid
to face the powerful of this earth
with your word of judgement,
in the sure knowledge
that nothing spoken in your name will be lost.
We make this prayer through Jesus Christ our Lord.

Year C
God, wellspring of life,
by the one Spirit you equip your people
with a rich diversity of many gifts.
Through these ministries, build up your Church,
and as we acknowledge Jesus to be Lord
by the power of the Holy Spirit,
make manifest among us the greatness of your glory.
We ask this through Jesus Christ our Lord.

Opening prayer

Years ABC
Lift up the light of your countenance on us, O God,
that we may be faithful to your commandments
and always do what is right and good.
We ask this through Jesus Christ our Lord.

Acclamations

Year A: John 1:29
V/. Behold, the Lamb of God:
who takes away the sin of the world.

Year B: John 1:51
V/. Jesus said, 'Very truly I tell you, you will see heaven opened:
and the angels of God ascending and descending upon the Son of Man.'

Year C: John 2:11
V/. Jesus did this, the first of his signs, in Cana of Galilee:
and revealed his glory.

Intercession

Years ABC
O God,
from every nation
you call your people together
and unite them in the Holy Spirit.
Equip your Church to serve the human family
as a life-giving leaven,
by drawing men and women
into a new birth as your beloved children.
We ask this through Jesus Christ our Lord.

Prayer over the Gifts

Years ABC
Lord, make us worthy to celebrate
the Supper of the Lord,
for as often as we do this
to celebrate his sacrifice,
the work of our redemption is made present.
We ask this through Jesus Christ our Lord.

Eucharistic Preface

Years ABC
It is truly right and just, our duty and our salvation,
always and everywhere to give you thanks,
Lord, holy Father, almighty and eternal God.

Through Christ, the fruit of the Virgin's womb,
you brought redemption to the human race,
whom sin and death had made its slave.
By your eternal Son you created all things;
now through his coming in human form
you have begun the new creation.
Where sin had triumphed over Adam
in the weakness of our mortal flesh,
your justice has prevailed and sin is overthrown
by your own Godhead in that same flesh incarnate.

And so, with angels and archangels
and with all the powers of heaven
we glorify your holy name
in this, their ageless hymn of praise: Holy . . .

For Year C – Preface based on the Gospel: John 2:1–11
This preface might be chosen in Year A on the Fourth Sunday of Epiphany and in Year B on the Third Sunday of Epiphany when that Gospel is read.

We lift up our hearts to you,
God eternal, true and faithful;
to you we offer thanks and praise
through Jesus Christ our Lord.

By a sign he gave at Cana in Galilee,
he announced his presence as the Messiah
and the outpouring of the Spirit that was to come.
By transforming water into wine,

he foretold the approach of that hour
when through his dying and rising
the whole creation would be made new
and he would unite his people to himself
in the eternal wedding feast.

And so, with all the powers of heaven,
we sing the hymn of this new creation,
praising you evermore and singing: Holy . . .

Prayer after Communion

Years ABC
Pour upon us, O God,
the Spirit of your love,
so that we who are nourished
by the one bread of heaven
may be made one body in Christ.
We ask this through Jesus Christ our Lord.

The Third Sunday of Epiphany

Scripture-related opening prayers

Year A
Upon the darkness of this world, O God,
the radiance of Christ has dawned,
a light for those who walked in the shadow of death.
Called by Christ, his first disciples
arose and followed him without delay.
Make us also ready witnesses to him,
and by the power of the cross
multiply among many nations
the number of those who acknowledge you
and celebrate your holy name.
We make this prayer through Jesus Christ our Lord.

Year B
God of all blessing,
in the bread and wine brought forth for Abraham our ancestor,
you foreshadowed the eternal marriage feast of the Lamb.
Clothe us in the bright works of justice,
that we may be worthy to sit at that banquet
and taste the new wine you have kept
as your gift for the age to come.
We make this prayer through Jesus Christ our Lord.

Year C
God, our greatest joy,
you give us this day of delight in your word
and celebration of our communion
as members of the body of Christ.
Let those you have anointed with your Spirit
be strengthened as the bearers of your good news,
so that your promise of life, justice and freedom
may be fulfilled in our days
to the furthest bounds of the world.
We make this prayer through Jesus Christ our Lord.

Opening prayer

Years ABC
Eternal God,
direct our actions
according to your purpose for us,
that we may abound in good works
in the name of your beloved Son,
who with you and the Holy Spirit is One God,
for ever and ever.

Acclamations

Year A: Matthew 4:17
V/. Jesus began to proclaim:
'Repent, for the kingdom of God is near.'

Year B: John 2:11
V/. Jesus did this, the first of his signs, in Cana of Galilee:
and revealed his glory.

Year C: Luke 4.18
V/. The Spirit of the Lord is upon me:
he has sent me to bring the good news to the poor.

Intercession

Years ABC
God of glory,
in Christ you have made yourself known
to every people and nation.
Watch over this work you have begun,
that your Church may remain faithful
in acknowledging your holy name.
We ask this through Jesus Christ our Lord.

Prayer over the Gifts

Years ABC
God of salvation,
before the world began you called us
to be brothers and sisters in Christ.
Make us holy through our fellowship at his table
and strengthen us in our calling.
We ask this through Jesus Christ our Lord.

Eucharistic Preface

Years ABC
It is truly right and just, our duty and our salvation,
to give you thanks and praise, O God,
and sing the wonders of your saving power.

You lift from us the weight of this world's troubles,
you console us with your many gifts;

but greatest of all is the joy of salvation
which you have bestowed upon us
by sending forth from the height of heaven
Christ your Son as our Redeemer.

Through Christ the choirs of angels
worship for ever before your glory.
With them you bid us join our voices
in this, their hymn of joyful supplication: Holy . . .

In Year B, the Preface given above for the Second Sunday of Epiphany, Year C, is an option as the Gospel is that of the Marriage at Cana, John 2:1–11.

Prayer after Communion

Years ABC
God, our provider,
grant that we who receive
your life-giving grace in the Eucharist
may always rejoice in your blessings.
Through Jesus Christ our Lord.

The Fourth Sunday of Epiphany

Scripture-related opening prayers

Year A
Most wise and glorious God,
in the foolishness of the cross
you made foolish the wisdom of this world.
Embolden your Church to boast only of you,
its holiness and strength,
and hasten the coming of that hour
when the waters that baptized us
will flow again as the new wine of your kingdom,

to manifest your glory in Jesus Christ,
who is alive and reigns for ever and ever.

Year B
God, before whom the forces of darkness flee,
you have given authority to your Christ
over every power that oppresses
and tortures the human spirit.
Renew in your Church the gospel that saves,
and let your people speak your words of liberation,
so that whatever enslaves or burdens humankind
may be overcome and banished
by the gentle rule of your Son,
who is alive and glorious for ever and ever.

Year C
Your praise, O God, reaches the ends of the earth,
for in Christ you have entered this world
and revealed to us your loving kindness.
Keep us faithful to the gifts of your Spirit,
and especially to that of charity,
so that we and those whose lives we touch
may see your salvation,
and come to know you face to face in Christ,
in whom we are fully known by you.
We make this prayer in his name
who is alive and reigns for ever and ever.

Opening prayer

Years ABC
Almighty God,
by grace alone you call us
and accept us in your service.
Strengthen us by your Spirit
and make us worthy of your call.
Through Jesus Christ our Lord.

Acclamations

Year A: John 2:11
V/. Jesus did this, the first of his signs, in Cana of Galilee:
and revealed his glory.

Year B: Mark 1:27b
V/. He commands even the unclean spirits:
and they obey him.

Year C : Luke 2:32
V/. A light for revelation to the gentiles:
and for glory to your people Israel.

Intercession

Years ABC
Father in heaven
the light of Jesus
has scattered the darkness of hatred and sin.
Called to that light
we ask for your guidance.
Form our lives in your truth,
our hearts in your love.
We ask this through Christ, our Lord.

Prayer over the Gifts

Years ABC
God, Creator of all,
we set your table with your own gifts to us.
As this bread and wine are prepared by human hands,
so shape our lives, we pray you,
so that in all things we may glorify your name.
We ask this through Jesus Christ our Lord.

Eucharistic Preface

Years ABC
We lift up our hearts to you,
God, the all-merciful and compassionate;
to you we offer thanks and praise
through Jesus Christ, your Son.

You give to the Church
his mysteries to celebrate
by which you work a wonderful exchange:
for our mortal nature you give immortal life,
for our existence in a universe of time
you bestow an eternal destiny,
for our slavery to the power of death
you give the glory of resurrection in Christ.

Through him, therefore,
we glorify your holy name
with all the heavenly beings,
singing without ceasing: Holy . . .

An alternative to this Preface might be that of the Presentation of Christ in the Temple given below, p. 19.

Prayer after Communion

Years ABC
You refresh and renew us, O God,
with the sacrament of salvation.
As we take up the mission you have given us
let this communion strengthen and increase
the faith you have planted in our hearts.
We ask this through Christ our Lord.

The Presentation of Christ in the Temple
Candlemas – 2 February

The origins of this festival lie in Jerusalem before the fifth century CE. *It was adopted by the Roman Liturgy during the seventh century. The celebration recalls the encounter of the infant Jesus with Simeon and Anna in the Temple. The meaning of this is that the Lord meets his people, who by the inspiration of the Holy Spirit recognize and acclaim him. Christ is revealed as the Light of nations, and so the tradition is to bless candles on this day.*

The Procession of Candles

The President greets the people as at the beginning of the Eucharist, introducing the ceremony with these or similar words:

Brothers and sisters in Christ, forty days ago we celebrated the feast of our Saviour's birth. Today, on the last day of that Christmas season, we remember the day when Mary and Joseph brought Jesus to the Temple. They came to present him in accordance with the law, but he had come to fulfil the prophecy that the Lord God would enter his Temple and greet those who believed in him.

Led by the Spirit, Simeon and Anna came to the Temple, recognized Christ as the One sent from God and proclaimed him joyfully. Called together by that same Holy Spirit, let us now welcome Christ, who comes to us in the breaking of bread, that we may without fear receive him when he comes in glory.

Let us pray.

After a pause for prayer, the priest blesses the candles using one of the following prayers.

Lord God,
source of unquenchable light,

on this day you revealed to Simeon
the light to enlighten all nations.
Bless these candles
and bless your people
who will carry them in praise of your name.
Make them walk in the path of goodness
until they reach the light which never fails.
Through Christ our Lord.

or:

Almighty God,
true light of the world
and source of light eternal,
shine upon the hearts of your faithful,
that all in this holy place
who are illuminated by these candles
may walk with joy towards the light of your glory.
Through Christ our Lord.

The candles may be sprinkled with holy water. The procession begins. Suitable songs are sung, which may include the Canticle of Simeon. The procession may conclude with the song Glory to God in the highest.

Scripture-related opening prayer

Years ABC
God of light,
your eternal Word
came to share our flesh and blood
and build us into a living temple
for your praise and glory.
Guide us by the Holy Spirit
to recognize and welcome your Christ
however he may present himself to us,
that on the day of his coming in judgement,

we may be found righteous in your sight,
and our lives may be accepted
as an offering pleasing to you.
We ask this through Jesus Christ our Lord.

Opening prayer

Years ABC
God of the Covenant,
whose Son accepted this human body
in order to destroy the power of death;
may we so present our bodies
as one in flesh and blood with him,
that by sharing the scandal of the cross,
we may be found worthy of eternal life.
We ask this through Jesus Christ our Lord.

Acclamation

Years ABC: Luke 2:32
V/. A light for revelation to the gentiles:
and for glory to your people Israel.

Intercession

Years ABC
Lord,
bless your people who seek your mercy,
and as you have planted in their hearts
the desire to be one with you,
so let that longing be fulfilled.
Through Jesus Christ our Lord.

Prayer over the Gifts

Years ABC
Almighty God,

accept the joyful praises of your Church,
and grant that your Son may shine in us
as the light that lightens every nation.
We ask this through Jesus Christ our Lord.

Eucharistic Preface

Years ABC
It is truly right and just, our duty and our salvation,
always and everywhere to give you thanks,
Lord, holy Father, almighty and eternal God.

Through the mystery of the Word made flesh
you have shone with a new and radiant light
upon the eyes of mind and heart.
Christ your Son, who is one with you eternally,
was this day presented in the Temple
and revealed by the Holy Spirit
as the glory of Israel and the light of all peoples.

And so, with all the angels we give you glory
in this, their joyful hymn of praise: Holy . . .

Prayer after Communion

Years ABC
Loving God,
make your grace perfect in us
through this holy feast,
and as you kept your promise to Simeon
that he would not see death
before he had welcomed the Messiah,
grant that we may go forth to meet the Lord,
and receive the gift of eternal life.
Through Jesus Christ our Lord.

Proper 1
The Sunday between 3 and 9 February inclusive
(if earlier than the Second Sunday before Lent)

Scripture-related opening prayers

Year A
God of integrity,
you demand that what we preach
be also that which we perform.
Let your Holy Spirit make manifest among us
the power of Christ crucified,
so that our words may season the world
with the taste of holy wisdom
and our works be true to that same justice
which you expect from those who worship you.
We make this prayer through Jesus Christ our Lord.

Year B
Eternal God,
your wisdom numbers the stars
and your care knows each of them by name.
Your compassion spans the heavens,
yet condescends even to this small earth.
Embrace us now as we stand before you;
give strength to our weakness,
open our mouths and stir up our spirits
to proclaim the gospel of your steadfast love,
in Christ, Jesus your Son, who is alive
and reigns for ever and ever.

Year C
You touch us, O God,
with the living fire of your holiness;
and though we are not worthy of it,
your grace has called us into your Church
to speak your word and tell of your glory

throughout the whole earth.
Keep us mindful of what you have wrought in us;
and make your Church a sign of reconciliation,
a place of welcome and friendship for all.
We ask this through Jesus Christ our Lord.

Opening prayer

Years ABC
Watch over your family, Lord,
with your unfailing care,
and as we rely completely on the hope of your grace
so may we be sheltered by your constant protection.
This we ask through Jesus Christ our Lord.

Acclamations

Year A: Matthew 5:16
V/. Let your light shine before others:
that they may give glory to your Father in heaven.

Year B: Mark 1:39
V/. Jesus went throughout Galilee:
proclaiming the message and casting out demons.

Year C: Luke 5:10b
V/. Jesus said to Simon, 'Do not be afraid:
From now on you will be catching people.'

Intercession

Years ABC
God, you only are good
and without you no one is found righteous.
Bid us, we pray, so to walk before you
as to be worthy of your great goodness.
We ask this through Jesus Christ our Lord.

Prayer over the Gifts

Years ABC
Creator God,
you provide food and drink
to sustain us on this earth.
Grant that this bread and wine
may be the sacrament of our eternal life.
Through Jesus Christ our Lord.

Eucharistic Preface

The Preface given below may be used on any of the Sundays between Candlemas and the pre-Lent Sundays.

It is truly right and just, our joy and our salvation,
always and everywhere to give you thanks,
Lord, holy Father, almighty and eternal God.

In your mercy, you so loved the world
that you sent your Son as our Redeemer,
desiring that he should be like us in all things but sin,
so that you might love in us what you loved in your Son.
By disobedience we lost your gifts of grace;
now through the obedience of Christ they are restored.

And so, with angels and all the hosts of heaven
we adore and glorify your holy name and say: Holy . . .

Prayer after Communion

Years ABC
Merciful God,
whose love draws us in to share
in the one bread and the one cup,
send us out to live as one in Christ
and to work for the salvation of all.
Through Jesus Christ our Lord.

Proper 2
The Sunday between 10 and 16 February inclusive
(if earlier than the Second Sunday before Lent)

Propers 2 and 3 are only used if there are more than four Sundays between 2 February and Ash Wednesday.

Scripture-related opening prayers

Year A
God of peace,
you call us to fulfil the spirit of your law
in righteousness, purity of heart and reconciliation.
Make us one in the bond of your charity;
take from our midst all enmity and malice,
so that by embracing one another in mutual forgiveness
we may offer at your altar
a gift that is worthy of your gospel.
We ask this through Jesus Christ our Lord.

Year B
Christ, our healer,
you touch the unclean, you love the unlovely,
you draw the outcast and despised
into the community of your friends.
As you have embraced us with such a tenderness,
strengthen our hands to welcome all
who through distress or rejection
have become our brothers and sisters.
This we ask of you, our Saviour
for ever and ever.

Year C
God, whose judgement confounds us,
you pronounce blessed those who are poor,
you promise to the hungry their fill of good things
and for mourners, the joy of mirth and laughter.

Save us from putting our trust
in the security afforded by this world,
and draw us to seek the blessings
promised to those who hope in you alone.
We make this prayer through Jesus Christ our Lord.

Opening prayer

Years ABC
Faithful God,
you promise to dwell with those
whose hearts are true and just.
Let the gift of your grace
make us worthy of your abiding presence.
This we ask through Jesus Christ our Lord.

Acclamations

Year A: Matthew 5:24
V/. 'Be reconciled to your brother or sister:
and then come and offer your gift,' says the Lord.

Year B: Mark 1:40
V/. A leper came to him begging him:
'If you choose, you can make me clean.'

Year C: Luke 6:20
V/. 'Blessed are you who are poor,' says the Lord:
'for yours is the kingdom of God.'

Intercession

Years ABC
Before we ask you, Lord,
you know what we need,
and so we pray to you:

accept our prayer and make us receptive
to everything you can give us,
through Jesus Christ our Lord.

Prayer over the Gifts

Years ABC
O God, at whose table
we are no longer strangers:
may we not refuse your call
through pride or fear,
but approach with confidence
to find our home in you
through Jesus Christ.

Eucharistic Preface

Years ABC
It is truly right and just, our duty and our joy,
always and everywhere to give you thanks and praise,
Lord, holy Father, almighty and eternal God.

On this, the day of the Lord,
you gather his disciples together
to celebrate the Passover of our redemption.
By your saving word you teach us,
and in the supper of the Lord
you feed us with the bread of heaven
and the cup that overflows with your Spirit.
In this, we come to know ourselves
as a people reborn to a living hope,
walking in one communion of love
and eagerly awaiting the coming of the Saviour.

And therefore, with angels and heavenly powers
we adore you and praise your holy name: Holy . . .

Prayer after Communion

Years ABC
Having feasted on heavenly food
we pray to you, Lord,
that we may always be hungry for that bread
by which alone we truly live.
Grant this through Christ our Lord.

Proper 3
The Sunday between 17 and 23 February inclusive
(if earlier than the Second Sunday before Lent)

Propers 2 and 3 are only used if there are more than four Sundays between 2 February and Ash Wednesday.

Scripture-related opening prayers

Year A
Holy God,
your outrageous love, revealed in Jesus,
constitutes the fullness of your law.
We beg you, by the gentle power of your Spirit,
to break the cycles of violence
that enslave and corrupt this world.
Free us to love our enemy and persecutor,
that we may recognize in them
the face of a brother and sister in Christ.
We ask this in his name,
who is with you and the Holy Spirit
one only God, for ever and ever.

Year B
Creator God,
in your bright wisdom
you bring forth gifts of new beginnings,
with grace and pardon for the past.

Forget our sins and make our lives
a faithful 'Amen' to your purposes;
so that, being sealed with your Holy Spirit,
we may both declare and imitate
your forgiveness and healing,
to the praise and glory of your name.
We make this prayer through Jesus Christ our Lord.

Year C
God, fount of life and wisdom,
open our ears and make us listen.
Draw us closer to those
whom now we know as enemies.
By your peaceful Spirit, enlighten our eyes
that we may perceive them no longer as foes,
but as your children, our brothers and sisters
in Christ, Jesus your beloved Son,
who with you and the Holy Spirit
is one living and true God, for ever and ever.

Opening prayer

Years ABC
Gracious God,
centre our hearts on what is true,
so that both in word and deed
we may fulfil your purposes for us.
We ask this through Jesus Christ our Lord.

Acclamations

Year A: Matthew 5:42
V/. 'Give to anyone who begs from you:
and do not refuse anyone who wants to borrow,' says the Lord.

Year B: Mark 2:12b
V/. They were all amazed and glorified God:
saying, 'We have never seen anything like this.'

Year C: Luke 6:31
V/. The Lord says: 'Do to others:
as you would have them do to you.'

Intercession

Years ABC
God of tender love,
you follow your people even when they stray.
Turn our hearts back to you
so that under your loving protection
we may persevere in your service.
Through Jesus Christ our Lord.

Prayer over the Gifts

Years ABC
God, our peace,
as we bring gifts to prepare your table,
reconcile us to one another
and unite us in your service and praise.
We ask this through Jesus Christ our Lord.

Eucharistic Preface

Years ABC
It is truly right and just, our joy and our salvation,
always and everywhere to give you thanks,
most gracious and loving God,
through Jesus Christ our Lord.

In the midst of human conflict
you turn our minds to long for peace.
For when your Spirit stirs our hearts,
enemies begin to speak to each other,
adversaries join hands in friendship
and nations seek the way of peace together.
Through your healing power

the love of peace quells violence,
mercy conquers hatred
and vengeance yields to forgiveness.

For all this we praise you,
joining our voices with the angels and powers of heaven
to sing their holy and ageless hymn: Holy . . .

Prayer after Communion

Years ABC
Faithful God,
grant that we may receive the fullness of salvation
whose promise we receive through the Eucharist.
Through Jesus Christ our Lord.

The Second Sunday Before Lent

Scripture-related opening prayers

Year A
Eternal God, by whose Creator Spirit
the formless void gave way to light,
the heavens and earth arose into being,
and humankind drew the first breath of life;
hasten now to fulfilment
your final purpose for the universe,
so that in Christ, your Creator Word,
all things may rise anew
and creation be brought from its bondage to decay
into the glorious liberty of your children.
We ask this through Jesus Christ our Lord.

Year B
How manifold are your works, O God!
In its wonder and beauty,
the universe declares your glory.

Now, in the greater wonder of redemption
you have shown the fullness of that glory
in Christ, your eternal Son.
Grant that your children,
brought forth to new birth in the blood of his cross,
may give true and faithful witness
to this new creation of your redeeming love.
We ask this through Jesus Christ our Lord.

Year C
In your wonderful creation, Lord God,
you fashioned humankind from the earth
and breathed into us the breath of life.
You determined that man and woman
should become one flesh.
Bless everything that establishes bonds of friendship
or kinship or charity in this world,
so that men and women, created to resemble you,
may find unity and be joined in your peace.
We ask this through Jesus Christ our Lord.

Opening prayer

Years ABC
In your Spirit, O God,
all reality holds together;
without you, it falls into corruption.
Do not abandon us to folly
but give us hearts that seek you
and at the last, joy in your new creation.
Through Jesus Christ our Lord.

Acclamations

Year A: Matthew 6:33
V/. 'Strive first for the kingdom of God and his righteousness:
and all these things will be given to you as well,' says the Lord.

Year B: John 1:12
V/. To all who received him, who believed in his name:
he gave power to become children of God.

Year C: Luke 8:25b
V/. They said: 'Who then is this:
that even the winds and water obey him?'

Intercession

Years ABC
God of compassion,
let your abundant blessings
enrich your people and keep them safe,
that they may rejoice in you
as the source and inspiration
of every good and righteous work.
Through Christ our Lord.

Prayer over the Gifts

Years ABC
God, our provider,
whose word has called us
to share in the table you have prepared;
give to us now, we pray you,
fitting words to sing your praise,
through Jesus Christ our Lord.

Eucharistic Preface

Years ABC
It is truly right and just, our duty and our delight,
always and everywhere to give you thanks,
Lord, holy Father, almighty and eternal God.

You are the origin of all that exists,
yours is the life in everything that breathes.

You clothe the heavens with glory
and fill the earth with your praise.
You formed us, men and women,
to embody your likeness,
and work with you as builders of your world
in the power of your Spirit,
through Jesus Christ our Lord.

Through Christ we acknowledge your greatness
in heaven's hymn of ceaseless praise: Holy . . .

Prayer after Communion

Years ABC
Merciful God,
at your saving banquet we are fed.
By this sacrament you nourish our life on earth;
so bring us, we pray, to your eternal life.
We ask this through Jesus Christ our Lord.

The Sunday Next Before Lent

Scripture-related opening prayers

Year A
In a bright cloud, O God,
you revealed the glory of your Christ,
and named him as your beloved Son.
As we listen to the Law and the prophets
let your Holy Spirit enlighten us,
that we may truly hear their witness
to the presence among us of the Word made Flesh,
who is one with you and the Holy Spirit,
now and always, for ever and ever.

Year B
Glorious God, on the holy mountain

you unveiled the splendour of your only Son
in whom is the fullness of the Law and prophets.
Shine in the heart of your people
and fan to flame in them
the gifts of your Holy Spirit,
that what they have heard and seen
they may go out and proclaim
as witnesses to the good news of your glory
in Jesus Christ, who lives for ever and ever.

Year C
You show us yourself, O God,
unveiled in the face of Jesus Christ.
Let the Holy Spirit free our minds and hearts
to grasp the sense of the Law and the prophets
so that as we contemplate Jesus in his passion
we may be able to proclaim him
as the crucified and living One,
whose glory is with you and the Holy Spirit,
for ever and ever.

Opening prayer

Years ABC
From the rising of the sun to its going down
your name is praised, O God,
for you have raised us from the dust and set before us
the vision of your glory.
As you bestowed upon us the dignity of a royal priesthood,
life up our hearts as we celebrate your praise;
through Jesus Christ our Lord.

Acclamation

Years ABC: Luke 9:35
V/. Then from the cloud came the voice of the Father:
'This is my Son, my Chosen: listen to him.'

Intercession

Years ABC
Guide your Church, we pray you, O Lord,
with your constant blessing from on high,
and as you chose us from the beginning
to stand in your presence and serve you,
so guide and govern your people,
that we may attain to the fullness
of the glory you have promised.
We ask this through Jesus Christ our Lord.

Prayer over the Gifts

Years ABC
Holy God,
let our prayer of thanksgiving
unite us to the praises of heaven,
in the glory of Christ,
who is alive for ever and ever.

Eucharistic Preface

Years ABC
It is truly right and just, our joy and our salvation,
always and everywhere to give you thanks,
holy Father, almighty and eternal God,
through Jesus Christ our Lord.

On the holy mountain,
Jesus made his glory known to his disciples,
to whom he had spoken of his coming death.
With Moses and Elijah as witnesses,
he revealed that the Christ had to suffer
in order to enter the glory of the resurrection.

And so, with joy, we echo on earth
the song of the angels of heaven
as they praise your glory without end:

Prayer after Communion

Years ABC
Gracious God,
you feed us in this sacrament
with the body and blood of your Son.
Rule us by your Spirit
that we may acknowledge you not only in word
but in action and in truth,
and so enter the kingdom of heaven.
Through Jesus Christ our Lord.

PART TWO

PROPER TEXTS FOR THE SUNDAYS BETWEEN TRINITY AND ALL SAINTS' DAY

On these Sundays, the Lectionary offers two alternative choices for the Old Testament reading: continuous or related. Related readings (on these Sundays usually the Old Testament, Psalm and Gospel) lend themselves better to Scripture-related opening prayers. Accordingly, for each related set, one is given.

For the continuous reading series, a collection of prayers is given covering Propers 4–25 of Years A, B and C. Some of these are original texts, but more are chosen for their 'fit' to the theme of the story. Not every Sunday on the continuous track will have a Scripture-related opening prayer, but if desired the same prayer can be used repeatedly.

The related collection of readings maintains a continuous reading of the Letters of Saint Paul. Except by coincidence, these seldom echo the Old Testament and Gospel choices. Accordingly, in a few cases where the Pauline reading is particularly noteworthy or well known, an alternative prayer is proposed, more closely linked to the second reading.

Gospel acclamation verses have been included.

A collection of prefaces is included at the end of the section, which are suitable for use where appropriate at any Sunday Eucharist. In Year C, Proper 10, when the Gospel of the Good Samaritan is read, a preface on that theme is included.

I. Collects and Other Prayers for Propers 4–25

Trinity Sunday

Scripture-related opening prayers

Year A
Into your name, O God, we are baptized,
by your grace redeemed
and in your tender love enclosed.
As you have come in search of us,
even so bestir us to seek you,
and in your threefold life
give us our true home for ever.
We ask this through Jesus Christ,
who is one with you and the Holy Spirit,
God, blessed for ever and ever.

Year B
Holy God,
let your Spirit sanctify the people
whom you have called into a new birth
in Jesus Christ your Son.
As we rejoice to be called your children,
so make us live
that we may be worthy of our calling and our name.
We ask this through Jesus Christ,
who is one with you and the Holy Spirit,
God, blessed for ever and ever.

Year C
God, source of all that exists,
in wisdom you created the universe
and by your holy breath of life
you sustain every human being.
As you so wonderfully reveal

your threefold name of Father, Son and Spirit,
so open our lives to yours
that we may glorify that holy name.
We ask this through Jesus Christ,
who is one with you and the Holy Spirit,
God, blessed for ever and ever.

Opening prayer

Years ABC
O God our mystery,
you bring us to life,
call us to freedom
and move between us with love.
May we so participate
in the dance of your Trinity,
that our lives may resonate with you,
now and for ever.

Acclamations

Year A: Matthew 28:19
V/. Alleluia, Alleluia, Alleluia.
R/. Alleluia, Alleluia, Alleluia.
V/. Go therefore and make disciples of all nations:
baptizing them in the name of the Father and of the Son and of the Holy Spirit.
R/. Alleluia, Alleluia, Alleluia.

Year B
V/. Praise to the Father, Son and Holy Spirit:
who was and is and is to come.

Year C: Te Deum
Father, of majesty unbounded,
your true and only Son, worthy of all praise,
the Holy Spirit, advocate and guide.

Intercession

Years ABC
God our Father,
you have called us to serve you and to love you;
recreate in us the image of your Son,
and direct our steps by the guidance of your Spirit,
so that our life may proclaim your praise
now and for ever and ever.

Prayer over the Gifts

Years ABC
God, source of every good gift,
as we enter the fellowship of your table
in praise and thanksgiving,
let this sacrament make us
an everlasting gift to you,
through Christ our Lord.

Eucharistic Preface

Years ABC
It is truly right and just,
our joy and our salvation,
always and everywhere to give you thanks,
Lord, holy Father, almighty and eternal God.

When sin had scattered your children,
You chose to gather them to yourself
through the blood of your Son and the power of the Spirit.
From the unity of your threefold being
your people take their being as your Church,
the body of Christ and the temple of the Spirit,
to the praise of your manifold wisdom.

And so, with angels and archangels
and with all the powers of heaven,

we glorify your holy name
in this, their ageless hymn of praise: Holy . . .

Prayer after Communion

Years ABC
Loving God,
as we receive this holy sacrament
and worship you, the undivided Trinity,
bring us to unity and wholeness of mind and body.
We ask this through Christ our Lord.

Proper 4
The Sunday between 29 May and 4 June inclusive
(if after Trinity Sunday)

Scripture-related opening prayers

Year A
God, our salvation,
you call us to live by your law of faith.
Let this law be written upon our hearts;
set it as a guardian at our lips
and bind it upon our minds.
Build us on the rock of Christ,
so that we may stand firm in time of trial,
and inherit the blessing you have promised
to those who put their trust in you.
We ask this through Jesus Christ our Lord.

Year B
God, our freedom,
you set aside this holy day
that we may remember our liberation
and rest from our labours.
Make this day a healing time
for all that is weary and withered in us,

and in our bodily celebration,
manifest among us the life of Jesus the risen One,
who is with you and the Holy Spirit,
one God, for ever and ever.

Year C
God of all being,
to whose gracious care no one is a stranger,
make us always rejoice in the breadth
of such an abundant love.
Let us never try to narrow
the scope of your grace,
but draw us to seek your peace and salvation for all,
that the whole earth may know your name
and declare your glory.
We ask this through Jesus Christ our Lord.

Opening prayer

Years ABC
O God,
whose providence will never fail,
remove from us whatever is harmful
and give us those things that will be for our good.
We ask this through Jesus Christ our Lord.

Acclamations

Year A: Matthew 7:21
V/. The Lord says: 'The one who does the will of my Father in heaven:
will enter the kingdom of heaven.'

Year B: Mark 2:27
V/. 'The Sabbath was made for humankind:
so the Son of Man is Lord of the Sabbath,' says the Lord.

Year C: Luke 7:9
V/. Jesus said: 'I tell you this:
not even in Israel have I found such faith.'

Intercession

Years ABC
In your kindness, Lord,
hear the intercession of your people.
Let no request be unanswered,
no prayer be made in vain,
but grant that what we ask in faith
we may receive from your generous love.
We ask this through Jesus Christ our Lord.

Prayer over the Gifts

Years ABC
God, giver of peace and true worship,
make our thanksgiving today
a fitting homage to your glory;
and as we share in your table,
unite us in your truth.
We ask this through Jesus Christ our Lord.

Prayer after Communion

Years ABC
God, provider of all good things,
you nourish us with the sacrament
of Christ's body and blood.
Rule our lives by your Holy Spirit
that we may profess your name
not in word alone,
but in action and truth
and so enter the kingdom of heaven.
We ask this through Jesus Christ our Lord.

Proper 5
The Sunday between 5 and 11 June inclusive
(if after Trinity Sunday)

Scripture-related opening prayers

Year A
God of compassion,
your mercy calls outcasts and sinners
to share in the work of Jesus.
Let that same power of love
subvert our righteousness and change our lives,
that we may put our trust, not in good works
but in your grace alone.
We ask this through Jesus Christ our Lord.

Year B
God, supreme and eternal good,
you sent your Son
to crush the power of Satan over the world
and to form us as brothers and sisters
in the one body of Christ.
Renew us day by day
with the power of the Holy Spirit,
so that in our struggle against evil
we may already know the victory
which your Son has gained for us,
for he is alive and reigns for ever and ever.

Year C
Eternal God, living and true,
you look with compassion on all people.
Renew the mission of your Church,
that death and oppression
may give way to life and freedom;
that heaviness of heart may turn to joy
and mourners be clothed with gladness,

for the glory of Jesus Christ, the risen One,
who is with you and the Holy Spirit
for ever and ever.

Opening prayer

Years ABC
God, who in the life and death of Jesus
have revealed your name to us;
let your Holy Spirit
draw us to him,
so that we may come
to know you more and more.
We ask this through Jesus Christ our Lord.

Acclamations

Year A: Matthew 9:13
V/. 'I desire mercy and not sacrifice,' says the Lord:
'For I have come to call not the righteous but sinners.'

Year B: Mark 3:35
V/. The Lord says: 'Whoever does the will of God:
is my brother and sister and mother.'

Year C: Luke 7:16
V/. A great prophet has arisen among us:
and God has visited his people.

Intercession

Years ABC
God, our light,
strengthen in our hearts
the faith kindled by your Spirit
and illuminate our minds by your word,
so that we may daily grow in faithfulness to you

and love of one another.
We ask this through Christ our Lord.

Prayer over the Gifts

Years ABC
Look kindly, Lord, upon our worship,
and since you welcome us at Christ's table,
so by your Spirit, make us grow in his love.
Through Jesus Christ our Lord.

Prayer after Communion

Years ABC
Lord, grant in your mercy
that your healing power in the Eucharist
may save us from going astray,
and lead us to what is right and good.
This we ask through Jesus Christ our Lord.

Proper 6
The Sunday between 12 and 18 June inclusive
(if after Trinity Sunday)

Scripture-related opening prayers

Year A
Gracious God,
you have displayed your steadfast love
in that while we were sinners, Christ died for us.
Let the Spirit of the risen One
make effective the ministry of your Church,
so that in speaking the good news
and in doing the works of Christ,
we may freely give what we have so freely received,
and so become a priestly people for your glory.
We ask this through Jesus Christ our Lord.

Year B
Great, O God,
is the power of your word
to plant and tend and grow a rich harvest.
Increase our faith in your provident care,
and as you call us
to take up the ministry of the gospel
so make us able to live no longer for ourselves,
but for the One who died and rose to life for us,
your Son, Jesus Christ,
who is one with you and the Holy Spirit,
for ever and ever.

Year C
God our Father,
you have brought us from sin to righteousness
through your gift of faith in Jesus.
Instruct us continually
in Christ's way of reconciliation,
so that we, whose sins you have forgiven,
may learn to imitate so great a love,
and as we have known the embrace of your mercy
so make us generous in showing mercy.
We ask this through Jesus Christ our Lord.

Opening prayer

Years ABC
God of all trust,
may we who confess your faith
prove it in our lives
with abundant joy,
outrageous hope
and dependence on nothing
but your word alone.
Through Jesus Christ, Amen.

Acclamations

Year A: Matthew 9:35
V/. Jesus went about all the cities and villages:
proclaiming the good news of the kingdom.

Year B: Mark 4:30–3
V/. The kingdom of God is like a mustard seed:
which becomes the greatest of all shrubs,
and the birds of the air can make nests in its shade.

Year C: Luke 7:47, 50
V/. Jesus said to the woman: 'Your sins are forgiven:
your faith has saved you, go in peace.'

Intercession

Years ABC
O God,
you bring us to new birth through your word of life.
Grant that by accepting that word
your Church may live by your truth
and show forth in our life together
the fruits of Christian love.
Through Jesus Christ our Lord.

Prayer over the Gifts

Years ABC
In bread and wine, O God,
you provide us with the food that sustains us
and the sacrament that gives us life.
Grant, we pray, that our minds and bodies
may always draw strength from your holy gift.
We ask this through Jesus Christ our Lord.

Prayer after Communion

Years ABC
Gracious God,
in the communion we have received
you foreshadow the union of all believers in you.
Grant that this sacrament
may bring unity and peace to your Church.
This we ask through Jesus Christ our Lord.

Proper 7
The Sunday between 19 and 25 June inclusive
(if after Trinity Sunday)

Scripture-related opening prayers

Year A
God of deliverance,
against whom evil cannot prevail,
stand together with those
who suffer the world's violence
because they speak your word,
and since they have acknowledged Christ
in the presence of others,
so may Christ acknowledge them as your own.
We ask this through Jesus Christ our Lord.

Year A – alternative
Grant, O God,
that as we are baptized
into the death of our Saviour Jesus Christ,
so by laying aside our old self
we may be buried with him,
and, being slaves no longer to sin,
may pass to a joyful resurrection in him,
who dies no more, but lives to you
both now and for ever and ever.

Year B
God, whose watchful care never sleeps,
through Christ, your eternal Word,
you bind the forces of the universe
and will not allow those you love to perish.
Bestow on your servants
the gift of enduring affliction with patience,
that our faith may commend your faithfulness to all.
We ask this through Jesus Christ our Lord.

Year C
Christ, to whom no one is an outcast,
you ordered the legion of demons
to depart from the one they had afflicted,
so that, clothed and in his right mind
he might be your apostle among his own people.
Look upon all who are baptized,
free them from evil and clothe them with your name,
so that they may tell of your wonders
and draw many into communion with you,
who are one with the Father and the Holy Spirit,
for ever and ever.

Opening prayer

Years ABC
God, our wisdom,
teach us always to reverence and love
your holy name that you have revealed to us;
for your guidance will never fail those
whom you establish in the firmness of your affection.
We ask this through Jesus Christ our Lord.

Acclamations

Year A: Matthew 10:39
V/. The Lord says: 'Those who find their life will lose it:
and those who lose their life for my sake will find it.'

Year B: Mark 4:41
V/. They were filled with great awe and said:
'Who then is this, that even the wind and the sea obey him?'

Year C: Luke 8:35b
V/. They found the man from whom the demons had gone:
sitting at the feet of Jesus, clothed and in his right mind.

Intercession

Years ABC
Today, O God,
you call us together to be your Church.
We thank you for the word,
the seed that you have sown in us,
and we pray that you will hear our prayer
made in faith and trust
for us and for all men and women,
through Jesus Christ our Lord.

Prayer over the Gifts

Years ABC
Accept, O God,
the sacrifice of praise,
and as you welcome us to your table
make us an offering pleasing to you,
through Jesus Christ our Lord.

Prayer after Communion

Years ABC
By the holy things we have shared, O God,
you nourish us and make us whole.
Let what we celebrate here bring us
to the fullness of your redemption.
Through Christ our Lord.

Proper 8
The Sunday between 26 June and 2 July inclusive

Scripture-related opening prayers

Year A
You promise your people, O God,
the reward and welcome
of those who speak in your name.
Endow us with the Holy Spirit of truth,
and let our speech and way of life
be consistent with our calling as prophets.
Enable us not only to announce your peace
but constantly to pursue it in all our actions.
We make this prayer through Jesus Christ.

Year B
God of steadfast love,
who created us for an eternal destiny;
you have shown your power to heal and give life
through the hand of Christ, your chosen One.
We ask you to raise up what is dead
and heal what is sick
in the life of your Church,
so that all may live in the joy and praise
for which you made us.
We ask this through Jesus Christ our Lord.

Year C
God, our heritage,
grant to your people grace
always to keep you in their sight,
so that, being guided by the Spirit,
those who follow you
may do so without condition or compromise,
in the assurance of faith
and the gentleness of compassion.
We ask this through Jesus Christ our Lord.

Opening prayer

Years ABC
God of truth,
by the grace of adoption
you have called us to be children of the light.
Do not let us be wrapped in darkness and error,
but make us rather stand out in the splendour of truth.
We ask this through Jesus Christ our Lord.

Acclamations

Year A: Matthew 10:40
V/. The Lord says 'Whoever welcomes you, welcomes me:
and whoever welcomes me welcomes the one who sent me.'

Year B: Mark 5:41–2
V/. Jesus took the child by the hand and said to her:
'Talitha, cum!' Which means 'Little girl, get up!'

Year C: Luke 9:51
V/. When the days drew near for him to be taken up:
Jesus set his face to go to Jerusalem.

Intercession

Years ABC
Stretch out over your Church, O God,
the ageless power of your strong right hand
and the gentle wisdom of the Holy Spirit,
that your people may worship and serve you
in confidence and peace.
We ask this through Jesus Christ our Lord.

Prayer over the Gifts

Years ABC
O God,
in the sacramental signs of bread and cup

you bring about the work of our redemption.
Grant that our worship and service
may be worthy of what we are celebrating.
Through Jesus Christ our Lord.

Prayer after Communion

Years ABC
Give us new life, O God,
through the holy gifts we have here received,
so that, united with you in perpetual love,
we may bring forth a lasting fruit of holiness.
Through Christ our Lord.

Proper 9
The Sunday between 3 and 9 July inclusive

Scripture-related opening prayers

Year A
Christ our Teacher,
gentle and humble of heart,
give us an attentive ear for your word,
and a mind ready to contemplate what we hear,
so that we may discover the wisdom hidden from the wise,
and manifest it before this generation
in all we say and do.
So shall you be glorified,
with the Father and the Holy Spirit,
now and always, for ever and ever.

Year B
God, our wisdom,
in the human weakness of your Christ
you have made the light of your Holy Spirit
shine forth in powerful deeds and words.

Tame our unbelief and hardness of heart,
that they hinder not his work among us,
and let us, in our own frailty,
know the perfecting of your power,
through Jesus Christ, who is with us,
till the ages end, for ever and ever.

Year C
Like a mother, O God,
you nurse the world with tender care,
and prepare it to receive your kingdom.
Bless all who labour in your harvest,
that they may rejoice to announce your peace
and not be afraid to declare
the coming of your judgement.
Let them rather rejoice in the hope
that their names are written in heaven.
This we ask through Jesus Christ our Lord.

Opening prayer

Years ABC
God of power,
who through the lowliness of your Son
raised up a fallen world;
grant to your people a holy gladness,
so that as you have rescued them from the slavery of sin
so you may bestow on them the joy of eternal life.
We ask this through Jesus Christ our Lord.

Acclamations

Year A: Matthew 11:28
V/. 'Come to me,' says the Lord, 'for I am gentle and humble in heart:
and you will find rest for your souls.'

Year B: Mark 6:12
V/. The Twelve went out and proclaimed that all should repent:
they anointed with oil many who were sick and cured them.

Year C: Luke 10:1
V/. The Lord appointed seventy others:
and sent them on ahead of him to every place he intended to go.

Intercession

Years ABC
Father of Jesus Christ,
open our hearts to your word
and to the power of the Spirit.
Give us love to discover your will
and strength to carry it out today;
for you are our light,
for ever and ever.

Prayer over the Gifts

Years ABC
Gracious God,
as we come to share in your table,
cleanse us and refashion us
with the new life of your kingdom.
Through Jesus Christ our Lord.

Prayer after Communion

Years ABC
God of abundance,
you fill us with every blessing.
Grant that we may hold fast your gifts of salvation
and never cease to sing your praise.
Through Jesus Christ our Lord.

Proper 10
The Sunday between 10 and 16 July inclusive

Scripture-related opening prayers

Year A
God, our freedom,
who raised Christ from the dead
to be the promise and the first fruits
of your Spirit dwelling within us;
set our minds on that same Spirit,
so that your word may take root in our hearts
and flourish unhindered
in lives that bear fruit with works of love.
We ask this through Jesus Christ our Lord.

Year B
God and Father,
in Christ your Son you reveal
the mystery of your will.
Grant courage and patience
to those who are persecuted
because of their witness to your law.
Keep us also faithful
to the Spirit who has sealed us as your own,
that we may live for your praise and glory.
We ask this through Jesus Christ, the Lord.

Year C
God of compassion,
your word is near, within our grasp,
as near as the neighbour whom you bid us love.
Let your Church be known
for its service to those most in need,
in imitation of Christ,
who came as the servant and healer of all.
We ask this in his name,

who is one with you and the Holy Spirit,
for ever and ever.

Opening prayer

Years ABC
As we celebrate today
the mystery of Christ's resurrection,
we ask you, gracious God,
to renew us by your Spirit.
Grant that we may live in thanksgiving
and in the hope of one day sharing
the fullness of joy in your presence,
for ever and ever.

Acclamations

Year A: Matthew 13:23
V/. 'Blessed are those who hear the word and understand it:
and bear fruit a hundredfold,' says the Lord.

Year B: Mark 6:29
V/. When John's disciples heard about it:
they came and took his body and laid it in a tomb.

Year C: Luke 10:33
V/. The Samaritan was moved with pity:
and bandaged his wounds, pouring oil and wine on them.

Intercession

Years ABC
Guide your Church, O God,
with wisdom from above,
and since from before the world was made
you have held us always in your presence,
so continue to lead your people

into the promised fullness of your glory.
We ask this through Jesus Christ our Lord.

Prayer over the Gifts

Years ABC
Lord, look kindly on us
as we prepare your table,
and grant to us who gather here
an increase in holiness and grace.
Through Christ our Lord.

Eucharistic Preface

Year C – Preface of the Good Samaritan
We lift up our hearts to you,
God of tender compassion;
to you we offer thanks and praise
through Jesus Christ your Son.

In his life among us,
Jesus went about doing good
and curing all kinds of sickness.
Still today he is the Good Samaritan
who tends the wounds of body and spirit,
who stands by us and pours out for our healing
the oil of consolation and the wine of hope renewed.
This is the gift which turns the darkness of our pain
into the dawning light of Easter,
the light of Christ, risen and glorified.

And so, with all the powers of creation,
we praise and bless your holy name: Holy . . .

Prayer after Communion

Years ABC
Receiving these holy gifts
we pray to you, Lord,

that each time we celebrate this mystery
the work of your salvation may grow within us.
Through Christ our Lord.

Proper 11
The Sunday between 17 and 23 July inclusive

Scripture-related opening prayers

Year A
God, whose care is for all people,
you show forbearance to your children,
because you give repentance for sins.
Let that mercy not leave us complacent,
but eager to learn patience and compassion;
and as you have made us righteous,
teach us also to be kind.
We ask this through Jesus Christ our Lord.

Year A – alternative
God, the source and end of all things,
in the resurrection of Christ
you reveal the first fruits of the Spirit,
the pledge of things to come.
Hear the sighs and groanings of creation,
and from its labour pains
bring freedom and glory to birth
for all your children.
We ask this through Jesus Christ
who is one with you and the Holy Spirit
for ever and ever.

Year B
O God, who reveal your threefold glory
as one communion of life and love,
in Christ Jesus you have broken down
the walls of partition that separate us.

Have compassion, we beg you,
on our divided world;
gather your disciples into unity,
reconcile nations and peoples.
Be glorified as the Shepherd of all,
Father, Son and Spirit, for ever and ever.

Year C
You come to us, O God,
with promises of good and gifts of grace.
Centre us on your presence
as you gather us for prayer,
so that whether we are active in service
or quiet in meditating on your word,
we may know that you alone
are the necessary choice for us,
and the fulfilment of our desire.
We make this prayer through Jesus Christ our Lord.

Year C – alternative
Gracious God,
your Creator Word
became part of your creation
by being born as one of us.
Through your Spirit,
let us praise him
as the firstborn of all beings
who unites all things in himself
and reconciles them all to you,
our God, blessed for ever and ever.

Opening prayer

Years ABC
Show kindness to your people, Lord,
and enrich us abundantly with your grace,
so that, firm in faith, secure in hope and constant in love,

we may keep your commandments with watchful care.
This we ask through Jesus Christ our Lord.

Acclamations

Year A: Matthew 13:43
V/. 'Then the righteous will shine like the sun:
in the kingdom of their Father,' says the Lord.

Year B: Mark 6:34
V/. Jesus had compassion on them:
because they were like sheep without a shepherd.

Year C: Luke 10:38–9
V/. A woman named Martha welcomed Jesus into her home:
her sister Mary sat at his feet and listened to what he was saying.

Intercession

Years ABC
Listen, O God,
to the prayers of your people,
as we commit ourselves to your care
and seek your blessing.
Protect and sustain us in this life
and make us ready for your eternal gifts.
We ask this through Jesus Christ our Lord.

Prayer over the Gifts

Years ABC
O God,
who in the self-offering of Christ
brought to an end the sacrifices of the old law;
bless what we bring to your table
as you blessed the righteous worship of Abel,

so that what each of us brings to praise you
may advance the salvation of us all.
We ask this through Jesus Christ our Lord.

Prayer after Communion

Years ABC
Lord, be close to us,
whom you have enriched with the gifts of heaven,
and grant that we may pass from our old ways
into new life according to the risen Christ,
who lives for ever and ever.

Proper 12
The Sunday between 24 and 30 July inclusive

Scripture-related opening prayers

Year A
God, treasury of all that is good;
like seed growing into a mighty tree
and yeast that makes the bread rise,
your kingdom is already working in our midst.
Kindle in us the desire to seek it,
and bestow the wisdom to discern it.
Make us single-minded to pursue it,
and give delight in the finding of it,
so that, with joy in its diversity,
we may announce its richness everywhere.
We ask this through Jesus Christ our Lord.

Year A – alternative
God, searcher of hearts,
your Spirit intercedes for all those
whom you have destined for your glory.
By that same Spirit, help our weakness;

continue to form us in the likeness of Christ,
that we may know the freedom of your children
and the assurance that nothing in creation
can separate us from your love.
We ask this through Jesus Christ our Lord.

Year B
God of abundance,
you open wide your hand
and fill every living being with plenty.
Sustain us with faith in your providence,
give us words for your praise and blessing
and make us generous
in sharing your bread
with the needy in body and spirit.
We ask this through Jesus Christ our Lord.

Year C
God, our lover,
tireless in seeking,
generous in giving:
grant to us a similar persistence
in forgiving those indebted to us
and as we knock so often at your door
make us keep our own doors open
for all who seek our welcome and our time.
We ask this through Jesus Christ our Lord.

Opening prayer

Years ABC
O God, whose law
is love of you and love of neighbour,
grant that we may keep this commandment
and so be found faithful in Christ,
who is alive for ever and ever.

Acclamations

Year A: Matthew 13:52
V/. Every scribe trained for the kingdom of heaven:
brings out of his treasure what is new and what is old.

Year B: John 6:11
V/. Jesus took the loaves and when he had given thanks:
he gave them to those who were seated.

Year C: Luke 11:9
V/. Jesus said: 'Ask and it shall be given to you, search and you will find:
knock and the door will be opened to you.'

Intercession

Years ABC
God, our teacher,
let your heavenly law instruct and shape our hearts,
that we may shun all wicked ways
and embrace the deeds and works of love
which your mercy has designed for us to do.
This we ask through Christ our Lord.

Prayer over the Gifts

Years ABC
We bring to your table, O God,
what your bountiful goodness has given us.
By this sacrament, make holy our life on earth
and bring us to the joy of life eternal.
We ask this through Jesus Christ our Lord.

Prayer after Communion

Years ABC
Lord, we share in the sacrament
which is the perpetual memorial of your Son's passion.

Grant, we pray,
that this gift of his wondrous love
may bring us to salvation.
Through Jesus Christ our Lord.

Proper 13
The Sunday between 31 July and 6 August inclusive

Scripture-related opening prayers

Year A
Compassionate God,
you know the hunger of this world
for bread that feeds the body and the spirit.
Let not those needs go unanswered,
but give courage to Christ's disciples
to place what little they have
into the hands of Christ,
at whose blessing it will be multiplied
and overflow in abundance for all to share.
We ask this through Jesus Christ our Lord.

Year B
God, whose gift is the true bread,
let the Spirit of holiness
teach and inspire your people,
so that with faith in your word
and believing in the One you have sent,
they may respond with understanding
to the hungers of this present age.
We make this prayer through Jesus Christ our Lord.

Year C
Eternal God,
you hold in your hands
the origin and destiny of all things,

and in Christ Jesus, the risen One,
you offer us the treasure of life eternal.
Keep before our minds
the remembrance of your mercy,
that we may set no store by this world's wealth.
Rather, let your grace make us rich
by what we freely give
to serve our brothers and sisters.
We ask this through Jesus Christ, our Lord.

Opening prayer

Years ABC
God of unceasing kindliness,
be present with us and bless your people.
We rejoice to acknowledge you as Creator and guide,
so now restore in us what you have created
and sustain the blessings you have restored.
We ask this through Jesus Christ your Son,
who is one with you and the Holy Spirit,
for ever and ever.

Acclamations

Year A: Matthew 14:20
V/. The crowd all ate and were filled:
and they took up what was left of the broken pieces, twelve baskets full.

Year B: John 6:27
V/. Jesus says: 'Work for the food that endures for eternal life:
which the Son of Man will give you.'

Year C: Luke 12:15
V/. 'Be on your guard against all kinds of greed:
for life does not consist in abundance of possessions,' says the Lord.

Intercession

Years ABC
Loving Father,
hear the prayers we offer
for all our brothers and sisters;
look with pity on those
whose work is hard and unrewarding
and support those who strive
for greater sharing and solidarity.
We ask you this
through Jesus, your Son, our Lord.

Prayer over the Gifts

Years ABC
Gracious God,
bless our fellowship at your table,
that we may become for you
an offering of worship in spirit and in truth.
Through Christ our Lord.

Prayer after Communion

Years ABC
Lord, be the constant shield of those
whom you renew by your gifts from heaven,
and as you never fail to care for us,
so make us worthy of everlasting redemption.
Through Jesus Christ our Lord.

Proper 14
The Sunday between 7 and 13 August inclusive

Scripture-related opening prayers

Year A
Gentle God,
whose quiet call is more disturbing

than earthquake, wind or fire;
you invite us to put our hand in yours
and trust in what we do not see.
Calm our fears,
catch us when we stumble
and give us the courage to persist
in following your purposes for us.
We ask this through Jesus Christ our Lord.

Year B
God, our provider,
who fed the prophet Elijah
in his wanderings and exile,
teach us to walk with greater confidence
in the ways of faith that lead to you.
Sustain us with the living bread,
Christ's gift of himself in word and sacrament,
so that we may reach our true home
as partakers in the feast of life eternal.
We ask this through Jesus Christ our Lord.

Year C
God our origin, our deepest desire,
uncover for us once more
the source of faith
which you have placed within our heart,
that we may live as a people who await
your unexpected coming,
and who work to find,
already in this present age,
the treasures that will never pass away.
We ask this through Jesus Christ our Lord.

Opening prayer

Years ABC
Almighty and eternal God,
taught by your Spirit we dare to call on you as Father;

fulfil in us the spirit of adoption,
that we may enter the inheritance you have promised.
We ask this through Jesus Christ our Lord.

Acclamations

Year A: Matthew 14:33
V/. Those in the boat worshipped Jesus and said:
'Truly, you are the Son of God.'

Year B: John 6:51
V/. Jesus says: 'I am the living bread that came down from heaven:
whoever eats of this bread will live for ever.'

Year C: Luke 12:34
V/. Jesus says: 'Where your treasure is:
there will your heart be also.'

Intercession

Years ABC
God of blessings,
source of every perfect gift,
keep us, we pray you, holy and blameless in your sight
and bestow on us the abundance of your grace.
Make us firm in your word of truth,
instruct us in the gospel of salvation
and fill our heart with love towards our neighbour.
This we ask through Jesus Christ our Lord.

Prayer over the Gifts

Years ABC
Receive us, O loving God,
as we prepare your table,
and by your transforming power

let us be found as one body and one spirit
in Christ, who is alive for ever and ever.

Prayer after Communion

Years ABC
God, our safety,
deliver us from evil as we share in your holy gift,
and make us stand firm in the light of your truth.
We ask this through Jesus Christ our Lord.

Proper 15
The Sunday between 14 and 20 August inclusive

Scripture-related opening prayers

Year A
God, whose gifts never fail,
whose love is never taken back,
make our faith strong and patient;
give us the wit to argue
and the persistence to keep asking,
that even in your silence we may know
the depths of your tender compassion.
We ask this through Jesus Christ, our Saviour.

Year B
In your eternal wisdom, O God,
you prepare for your Church
the living bread which is Christ's body
and the cup of communion in his blood.
Look upon your people gathered here;
let your Spirit fill this assembly
that we may draw others to your holy table,
to be nourished with this food and drink
of life and resurrection in Christ,
the risen One, who lives for ever and ever.

Year C
God of salvation,
in the power of the cross
you reveal your judgement on the world
and the kingship of Christ, the crucified.
May we not refuse to accept
the challenge which he offers,
so that being baptized into his death
we may run with perseverance
in the costly way that he has set before us,
looking always to him, the risen One,
who lives for ever and ever.

Opening prayer

Years ABC
Faithful God,
you have established with us
your covenant of love.
Remember your promise
fulfilled in your anointed Son Jesus Christ
and count us worthy to stand in his strength alone;
who with you and the Holy Spirit
lives and reigns for ever and ever.

Acclamations

Year A: Matthew 15:28
V/. Jesus answered her, 'Woman, great is your faith:
let it be done for you as you wish.'

Year B: John 6:56
V/. The Lord says: 'Those who eat my flesh and drink my blood:
abide in me and I in them.'

Year C: Luke 12:49
V/. Jesus said: 'I came to bring fire to the earth:
and how I wish it were already kindled.'

Intercession

Years ABC
God of wonders,
kindle in the heart of your Church
the fire of the Holy Spirit,
that we may be dedicated anew
to the mission you have entrusted to us.
We ask this through Christ our Lord.

Prayer over the Gifts

Years ABC
At this holy table, O God,
you share your life with us.
Make us, we pray, worthy
of this inexpressible blessing,
through Christ our Lord.

Prayer after Communion

Years ABC
God of mercy,
through this holy Eucharist
you make us one body with Christ.
Create us in his likeness here on earth
that we may share his fellowship in heaven,
where he lives and reigns for ever and ever.

Proper 16
The Sunday between 21 and 27 August inclusive

Scripture-related opening prayers

Year A
Father in heaven,
who gave to Simon Peter
the faith to profess Jesus as the Messiah;
build up your Church on that same faith,
and as you desire us
to be members one of another,
give us strength in the many gifts
which bind us as one body in Christ.
We ask this in his name,
who is our Saviour and our peace,
now and for ever.

Year B
God, in whom we abide continually,
save us from losing heart
when your teaching is hard to understand
or difficult to put into practice.
Fill us rather with the life-giving Spirit,
so that, knowing you to be so near to us,
we may gladly serve and honour you,
who alone possess the word of eternal life.
We make this prayer through Jesus Christ our Lord.

Year C
Today, O God our deliverer,
you raised up our Saviour Jesus Christ
and set us free from the power of death.
Let all we do this day
be directed to your glory
and to the freedom of those
who are oppressed or burdened.

We ask this in the name of Christ,
for with him and the Holy Spirit
you are one God, blessed for ever and ever.

Opening prayer

Years ABC
Lord God,
you have created us in your own image
to find freedom in a love that knows no bounds.
Lead us further today along this path of freedom
to which you call us
through Jesus, your beloved Son, our Lord.

Acclamations

Year A: Matthew 16:15–16
V/. Jesus asked his disciples; 'Who do you say I am?'
Simon Peter answered: 'You are the Messiah, the Son of the living God.'

Year B: John 6:68
V/. Simon Peter said: 'Lord, to whom shall we go?
You have the words of eternal life.'

Year C: Luke 13:17
V/. The entire crowd was rejoicing:
at all the wonderful things Jesus was doing.

Intercession

Years ABC
Father in heaven,
from the days of Abraham and Moses
until this gathering of your Church in prayer,
you have formed a people in the image of your Son.
Bless this people with the gift of your kingdom,

that we may serve you with our every desire
and love one another as you have loved us.
We ask this through Jesus Christ our Lord.

Prayer over the Gifts

Years ABC
Gracious God,
who by the offering of Christ made once for all
adopted a people as your own;
bestow now in grace upon your Church
your gifts of unity and peace.
We ask this through Christ, our Lord.

Prayer after Communion

Years ABC
God of mercy,
complete within us your healing work,
and so transform and strengthen us
that our lives and actions may give you joy.
We ask this through Christ, our Lord.

Proper 17
The Sunday between 28 August and 3 September inclusive

Scripture-related opening prayers

Year A
Father of glory,
in great love you brought your only Son
through suffering to resurrection.
Grant to all who have been baptized into his death
that they may not refuse the cost of discipleship
when it is asked of them,
but that, in giving their life for your sake,

they may receive it again
as your gift of life eternal.
We ask this through Jesus Christ,
who is one with you and the Holy Spirit
for ever and ever.

Year B
Come close to us, O God,
and with your word of truth
purify the intentions of our hearts.
Let us walk in your law of liberty
as doers who act and are blessed in their doing,
so that what we profess with our lips
we may carry out in our lives
for the sake of your praise and glory,
through Jesus Christ our Lord.

Year C
God of the lowly,
whose eternal Son
assumed the condition of a servant
and welcomed the outcast and poor;
let such a humility be exalted among us.
Let us not refuse those whom the world rejects
but have eyes to discern your presence in them
and hope of their fellowship
in the resurrection of the dead.
We ask this through Jesus Christ our Lord.

Opening prayer

Years ABC
O God unknown,
in our mother's womb
you formed us for your glory.
Give us a heart to long for you,
grace to discern you,

and courage to proclaim you;
through the one whom you loved
before the foundation of the world,
our Saviour Jesus Christ.

Acclamations

Year A: Matthew 16:28
V/. Jesus said: 'Truly, I tell you there are some who will not taste death:
before they see the Son of Man coming in his kingdom.'

Year B: Mark 7:21–3
V/. Jesus said: 'It is from the human heart that evil intentions come:
all these things come from within and they defile.'

Year C: Luke 14:11
Jesus says: 'All who exalt themselves will be humbled:
and those who humble themselves will be exalted.'

Intercession

Years ABC
Eternal God, source of all peace,
you call your children to live together as one family.
Give us grace to learn your ways
and to do your will,
that we may bring your justice and peace to all people,
by the power of Jesus Christ,
our Lord for ever and ever.

Prayer over the Gifts

Years ABC
We have sought you, Lord Jesus,
in our prayer;

may we recognize you in the breaking of bread,
and find you in all who come our way this day,
you whom we shall one day know fully,
for ever and ever.

Prayer after Communion

Years ABC
God most high,
we have been fed at your table
with the bread of heaven.
Strengthen your love in our hearts
and inspire us to serve you in our brothers and sisters.
Through Christ our Lord.

Proper 18
The Sunday between 4 and 10 September inclusive

Scripture-related opening prayers

Year A
God, in whose holy name
we are gathered together,
make your people one
in faith with each other
and keep them united in the charity of Christ,
so that the things we bind and loose on earth
you yourself may judge worthy
to be bound and loosed in heaven.
We ask this through Jesus Christ, our Lord.

Year B
Be present, O God,
like waters in a desert,
and make fruitful
the ministry to which you call us.

Let those who cannot perceive you,
those who cannot find words to pray,
those oppressed by evil and sin,
find among your people
healing for their brokenness
and freedom from their bonds,
through Christ, who is our Saviour,
for ever and ever.

Year C
Christ, our only surety,
through your inspiration
we dare to call ourselves your disciples.
By your grace enable us
to carry the cross and follow you,
and in our struggle to persevere
let the Holy Spirit supply us freely
from the wellspring of eternal life.
We ask this of your faithful love,
both now and for ever and ever.

Opening prayer

Years ABC
God our Father,
who redeemed us and made us your children,
look upon us, who put our faith in Christ;
make us truly free
and bring us to the inheritance you promised.
We make this prayer through Jesus Christ our Lord.

Acclamations

Year A: Matthew 18:20
V/. Jesus says: 'Where two or three are gathered in my name:
I am there among them.'

Year B: Mark 7:37
V/. They said: 'He has done all things well:
he makes the deaf to hear and the mute to speak.'

Year C: Luke 14:27
Jesus says: 'Whoever does not carry the cross and follow me:
cannot be my disciple.'

Intercession

Years ABC
Lord God, King of the universe,
you show the bright glory of your reign
in acts of mercy and enduring love:
raise the spirits of the downcast
and restore those who have fallen away,
that your Church may continually sing of your saving help,
through Jesus Christ our Lord.

Prayer over the Gifts

Years ABC
Lord God,
let our praises come before you,
so that, united in faith,
we may worship in spirit and in truth,
through Jesus Christ our Lord.

Prayer after Communion

Years ABC
God of word and sacrament,
you nourish your people and give them life.
Grant that these gifts of your Son
may make us grow in holiness
so that we may be worthy to share his life for ever.
Through Jesus Christ our Lord.

Proper 19
The Sunday between 11 and 17 September inclusive

Scripture-related opening prayers

Year A
God, our righteousness,
high as heaven is your mercy,
for you do not retain anger for ever.
Through the word of Jesus,
challenge our ways.
Through the Spirit of Jesus,
expel from us all wrath and resentment,
so that we who ask mercy for ourselves
may forgive our brother and sister from the heart.
We ask this through Jesus Christ, our Saviour.

Year B
Gracious God,
open our ears to your word
that we may listen and be taught as your disciples.
Grant that our faith in Jesus as the Christ
may not grow fearful at the sight of the cross,
but may remain steadfast in him,
and take flesh in works of charity for those in need.
We make this prayer in his name,
our Saviour for ever and ever.

Year C
Patient God,
whose angels rejoice
over the repentant sinner,
remember your covenant of mercy
and stir up among us on earth
a desire to share the gladness of heaven,
so that your Church may be a place of welcome
for all who turn from sin
to seek your tender love.

We ask this through Jesus Christ,
who intercedes for us now and always,
for ever and ever.

Opening prayer

Years ABC
Creator God, Ruler of all that is,
listen to our prayer;
grant that we may serve you with an undivided heart
and in your service, come to know your mercy.
We ask this through Jesus Christ our Lord.

Acclamations

Year A: Matthew 18:21–2
V/. Jesus said to Peter: 'Forgive, not seven times:
but, I tell you, seventy-seven times.'

Year B: Mark 8:31
V/. Jesus began to teach them that the Son of Man must suffer:
and after three days rise again.

Year C: Luke 15:10
V/. The Lord says: 'There is joy in the presence of the angels of God:
over one sinner who repents.'

Intercession

Years ABC
Almighty God,
you call your Church to witness
that you have reconciled all things in Christ.
Help us so to proclaim the good news of your love
that all who hear it may turn to you.
We ask this through Jesus Christ our Lord.

Prayer over the Gifts

Years ABC
Holy God,
grant that as we are reconciled at this table,
so we may seek wholeness for our broken world.
We ask this through Christ our Lord.

Prayer after Communion

Years ABC
Almighty God,
through this sacrament
take possession of us, body and soul,
so that our lives may respond
not to our own will,
but to the working of these holy gifts.
We ask this through Jesus Christ our Lord.

Proper 20
The Sunday between 18 and 24 September inclusive

Scripture-related opening prayers

Year A
Confront us, O God,
with that absolute and tender care
which you extend to every human being.
In our dealings together
do not let us insist on justice to the exclusion of mercy,
nor pursue equity to the detriment of compassion,
but as we have known your graciousness,
so make us exercise to others
that mercy you have shown us
in Christ, Jesus your Son,
our Saviour, for ever and ever.

Year B
God and Father,
who gave your Son, the Saviour of all,
that he might become the servant of all;
grant that through Christ's cross,
the world may aspire
to a new justice,
a welcome for the outcast,
compassion for little ones
and a communion of love for all people.
So will your peace be cultivated
and the harvest of your justice shared,
through Christ, who is our reconciliation,
for ever and ever.

Year C
Eternal God,
whose providence has placed us
both in this age and in the age to come,
grant us the wisdom
to use the goods of this world for your glory
and in the service of one another,
so that at the last we do not fail to reach
the blessings that abide for ever.
We make this prayer through Jesus Christ our Lord.

Opening prayer

Years ABC
God, our justice,
you have founded all your holy law
on love for you and for our neighbour.
Make us keep these two commandments,
that we may come to eternal life.
We make this prayer through Jesus Christ our Lord.

Acclamations

Year A: Matthew 20:16
V/. Jesus says: 'The last will be first:
and the first will be last.'

Year B: Mark 9:35
V/. Jesus said to the Twelve: 'Whoever wants to be first;
must be last of all and servant of all.'

Year C: Luke 16:13
The Lord says: 'No one can serve two masters:
you cannot serve God and wealth.'

Intercession

Years ABC
Father,
your love never fails.
Hear our call,
keep us from every danger
and provide for all our needs.
We make this prayer through Jesus Christ our Lord.

Prayer over the Gifts

Years ABC
Receive us, O God
as we prepare your table,
and as you have called us to assemble here,
so gather us into the mystery
which we profess in thanksgiving and praise.
We ask this through Christ our Lord.

Prayer after Communion

Years ABC
God of unfailing help,
support those you nourish with this sacrament,

that we may experience
the power of your redeeming love
both in this Communion
and in the conduct of our lives.
This we ask through Jesus Christ our Lord.

Proper 21
The Sunday between 25 September and 1 October inclusive

Scripture-related opening prayers

Year A
God of truth,
you look not on the promises we make
but on our keeping of what was promised.
Renew us, we pray you, in heart and spirit,
so that what was affirmed and pledged in our baptism
may be fulfilled in lives of faith and love.
We ask this through Jesus Christ our Lord
whose glory is one with you and the Holy Spirit
one God, for ever and ever.

Year A
Lord our God,
to carry out your will
your only Son became as one of us,
submitting himself even to death,
and in his obedience you have shown your glory.
Let his mind be in us,
that we may serve one another
and consider each other's interests
before thinking of our own.
We ask this in his name,
who is glorified with you and the Holy Spirit
for ever and ever.

Year B
God of peace,
you display your works of healing and power
irrespective of the boundaries we erect.
Grant us the Spirit of discernment
that we may recognize your sovereign freedom,
rejoice in your boundless grace
and be watchful over our own words and actions.
We ask this through Jesus Christ our Lord.

Year C
Christ, risen from the dead,
whose hands reach out to us
in the person of the needy and outcast;
bestir us both in thought and in deed
to be mindful of those who seek our compassion,
so that your justice may be done,
your beloved poor be served,
and your people enter into eternal life.
We humbly ask this of you,
the fountain of all mercy
who live and reign for ever and ever.

Opening prayer

Years ABC
Father in heaven,
the light of your Christ
has scattered the darkness of hatred and sin.
Called to that light
we ask for your guidance.
Form our lives in your truth,
our hearts in your love.
We ask this through Jesus Christ our Lord.

Acclamations

Year A: Matthew 21:23
V/. When Jesus entered the Temple:
the chief priests and elders came to him as he was teaching.

Year B: Mark 9:40
V/. Jesus said to John:
'Whoever is not against us is for us.'

Year C: Luke 16:31
V/. 'If they do not listen to Moses and the prophets:
neither will they be convinced even if someone rises from the dead.'

Intercession

Years ABC
Grant, O merciful God,
that your Church,
being gathered into unity by the Holy Spirit,
may show forth your power among all peoples,
to the glory of your name;
through Jesus Christ our Lord.

Prayer over the Gifts

Years ABC
Open our lips, O God,
in praise and thanksgiving,
and as we gather at your table,
open also for us the living streams of your blessing.
We ask this through Christ our Lord.

Prayer after Communion

Years ABC
Gracious God,
through this holy sacrament

restore us in mind and body,
so that we who by proclaiming the death of Christ
are united with him in his passion,
may become co-heirs with him in glory,
who lives and reigns for ever and ever.

Proper 22
The Sunday between 2 and 8 October inclusive

Scripture-related opening prayers

Year A
Turn again, O God of hosts,
turn us again, and we shall live.
In the light of your countenance
reveal the pride and self-centredness
that keep us from your kingdom.
Renew us by your Spirit
that we may hear the word of Christ,
and, built on him as the cornerstone,
may bring forth the fruit of your good work in us.
We ask this in his name, Jesus Christ our Lord.

Year B
God of community,
in your threefold wisdom you have ordained
that it is not good for us to be alone.
Restore to the children of Adam and Eve
the holiness and harmony
with which you endowed the beginning of creation,
that those united in marriage
may remain faithful to each other,
and that every bond of friendship and affection
may be blessed, confirmed and perfected
through Jesus Christ, in the Holy Spirit,
for ever and ever.

Year C
Amid this world's violence and destruction
and having but a little faith,
we come to you, God our refuge.
Allow us to share your vision
and grant us the patience to await its allotted time.
Make us trust in your prevailing will
that we may commit our destiny to you,
be confident in our witness to your truth,
and faithful in our task of service.
We ask this through Jesus Christ our Lord.

Opening prayer

Years ABC
Gracious God,
guide us by the light of your truth
through a world filled with lights contrary to your own,
and as by your gift we have the name of Christian,
so make us in truth what you have called us to be.
We ask this through Jesus Christ our Lord.

Acclamations

Year A: Matthew 21:42
V/. The stone that the builders rejected:
has become the cornerstone.'

Year B: Mark 10:7
V/. 'A man shall leave his father and mother and be joined to his wife:
and the two shall become one flesh.

Year C: Luke 17:5
The Lord says: 'When you have done all you were ordered to do, say this:
"We are worthless servants; we have done only what we ought to have done."'

Intercession

Years ABC
Lord, we pray that your continual encouragement
will support the worship and life of your Church,
that she may draw strength from your gifts in this present age
and reach at last the blessings of eternal life.
We ask this through Christ our Lord.

Prayer over the Gifts

Years ABC
Grant to us, Lord God,
that we, following the command of Christ,
may find at this table
the fullness of your redeeming work.
We ask this through Christ our Lord.

Prayer after Communion

Years ABC
Almighty God,
may the sacrament we share
feed us and fire our senses with your joy,
so that we may be transformed
into that which we have received.
Through Christ our Lord.

Proper 23
The Sunday between 9 and 15 October inclusive

Scripture-related opening prayers

Year A
God, to whose eternal banquet
the whole world is summoned as your guest;
keep us mindful of your call to holiness,
and clothe us in the practice of good works,

so that we, the last and least
of those you have invited,
may not come unprepared,
but may be welcome at your table
and rejoice in your salvation.
We make this prayer through Jesus Christ,
your Son, our Saviour for ever and ever.

Year B

God, all-wise and all-just,
you have shown us your commandments
and you make it possible for us to obey them.
Free us from the snare of this world's goods,
that we may recognize in the face of Jesus
the love which calls us to discipleship
and to the surrender of all other wealth
for the priceless treasure of your kingdom.
We ask this in his name,
Christ Jesus, your Son and our high priest,
for ever and ever.

Year C

God of wholeness,
at whose word the sick are made well,
the troubled made serene and sinners forgiven,
let your Church never cease to thank you
for salvation of mind and body,
and let our joy overflow
in service of our neighbour.
We ask this through Jesus Christ,
the faithful witness for ever and ever.

Opening prayer

Years ABC

With your unwearied grace, O God,
go before us and follow us,

and make us eager
in the practice of good deeds.
We ask this through Jesus Christ our Lord.

Acclamations

Year A: Matthew 22:8
V/. The King said to his servants, 'Go into the main streets:
and invite everyone you find to the wedding banquet.'

Year B: Mark 10:23
V/. Jesus said: 'How hard it is to enter the kingdom of God:
for mortals it is impossible, but for God all things are possible.'

Year C: Luke 17:19
The Lord said to the cleansed leper: 'Get up and go on your way:
your faith has made you well.'

Intercession

Years ABC
We pray you, Lord,
let your Church rejoice
in the rich treasure of your heavenly gifts,
that by your grace it may remain faithful in Christ
and receive at last the blessing of your kingdom.
We ask this through Christ our Lord.

Prayer over the Gifts

Years ABC
God of constant love,
in the Eucharist you renew the covenant
made once with us in baptism.
As you are faithful in all things,
may we also be faithful to our calling.
We ask this in the name of Jesus the Lord.

Prayer after Communion

Years ABC
God of majesty,
receive our humble prayer:
and as you give us Communion
in the body and blood of your Son,
so make us partakers of his divine nature,
for he is alive and reigns for ever and ever.

Proper 24
The Sunday between 16 and 22 October inclusive

Scripture-related opening prayers

Year A
God, whose likeness we bear,
you and you alone
are the source of our being,
the strength of our life
and the fulfilment of our hope.
Focus our hearts and wills on your gospel
that we may render to you
the worship you deserve
and offer to our neighbour
the service that you command.
We make this prayer through Jesus Christ,
your Son and our Saviour for ever and ever.

Year B
Christ, who as a servant
emptied yourself of glory
and carried all our afflictions;
teach us this obedience:
that since in baptism
we are united to your sufferings,

so, through sharing the burdens of the needy
and standing as witnesses to your justice,
we may be found in that eternal life
which you have with the Father and the Holy Spirit
for ever and ever.

Year C
Hidden God,
with whose mystery we struggle
and whose face we long to see,
do not allow us to lose heart before you,
despite our wavering faith;
but in your compassion, deign to be conquered
by the insistent prayer of those
who seek your blessing and your strong help.
We ask this through Jesus Christ
for in his arms we are held fast
for ever and ever.

Opening prayer

Years ABC
Almighty God,
create in us a will and purpose
that accords at all times with your own,
and so direct the course of our lives
that we may serve you with undivided hearts.
We ask this through Jesus Christ our Lord.

Acclamations

Year A: Matthew 22:21
V/. Jesus said: 'Give to the emperor the things that are the emperor's:
and to God the things that are God's.'

Year B: Mark 10:45
V/. Jesus said: 'The Son of Man came not to be served but to serve:
and to give his life a ransom for many.'

Year C: Luke 18:8b
V/. 'When the Son of Man comes,' says the Lord:
'will he find faith on earth?'

Intercession

Years ABC
O God, by whose Holy Spirit
a multitude of people are gathered
and united in witness to your Son,
grant that your Church
may walk in faith with the human family
as a force to renew all things in Christ,
who lives and reigns for ever and ever.

Prayer over the Gifts

Years ABC
Bring us, O gracious God,
to praise you at your table
with free and generous hearts,
so that we may be set free from sin
to worship you in spirit and in truth,
through Christ our Lord.

Prayer after Communion

Years ABC
We pray you, Lord,
let our handling of heavenly things
make us receptive to your presence,

so that, being blessed by you in this present age,
we may be prepared for the blessings of the age to come.
Through Christ our Lord.

Proper 25
The Sunday between 23 and 29 October inclusive

Scripture-related opening prayers

Year A
Holy God,
whose justice is without partiality
and whose mercy embraces all that live,
remove all trace of injustice
from the hearts of your people,
that through love of you and of neighbour,
hatred may yield to forgiveness
and quarrels give place to reconciliation.
We ask this through Jesus Christ,
your Son and our Lord, for ever and ever.

Year B
God of wonders,
whose purpose is to save the lost
and bring back with rejoicing
those who went away in tears,
have pity on us and open our eyes.
Restore to your Church
the vision of a world made new,
and give to your people the strength
to take up again the work of Christ
in announcing the coming of your kingdom.
We ask this through Jesus Christ our Lord.

Year C
God, before whom none can justify themselves
or plead any good of their own,

hear and correct our prayer,
and when we are tempted to praise ourselves
or make judgements on our neighbour,
show us how hollow is our claim to righteousness
and give us grace to ask for your mercy.
We make this prayer through Jesus,
our holiness and our peace,
who is one with you and the Holy Spirit,
for ever and ever.

Opening prayer

Years ABC
God, fount of all being,
let the gift of your life
continue to grow in us,
drawing us out of death
into faith, hope and love.
Keep us alive in Christ Jesus,
watchful in prayer and true to his teaching
until the day when your glory is revealed.
We ask this in his name,
who lives for ever and ever.

Acclamations

Year A: Matthew 22:44
V/. 'The Lord said to my Lord:
'Sit at my right hand.'

Year B: Mark 10:51
V/. Jesus said to the blind man, 'What do you want me to do for you?'
The blind man said to him, 'My teacher, let me see again.'

Year C: Luke 18:14
V/. The tax collector stood beating his breast and saying:
'Lord, be merciful to me, a sinner.'

Intercession

Years ABC
God of all,
through the gift of your Spirit
you have united your people
in the confession of your name.
Lead us, by the same Spirit,
to show to the whole earth
one mind in faith
and one faith for justice,
through Jesus Christ our Lord.

Prayer over the Gifts

Years ABC
Look upon us, O God,
as we prepare your holy table,
and grant that our service
may be directed to your glory and praise,
through Christ our Lord.

Prayer after Communion

Years ABC
Lord,
may these holy gifts accomplish within us
the salvation they embody,
so that what we do in sign and symbol
we may receive in fullness and in truth.
Through Christ our Lord.

II. Collects Related to the Old Testament Continuous Reading Option

Year A

In Year A, the continuous reading begins in Proper 4 with the story of Noah, and follows the patriarchal history through until the sojourn in Egypt. It follows the story of the Exodus from the birth of Moses until his death on the threshold of the Promised Land.

The following Collects reflect aspects and incidents of the narrative:

Proper 4: Genesis 6:9–22; 7:24; 8:14–19

Noah
God of steadfast love,
in the waters of the deluge
you swept away the world's corruption,
and in the saving flood of baptism
you give us a new beginning in holiness.
Keep us faithful to your covenant,
purify all that is corrupt in us;
make us live according to your justice
and pursue the things that make for peace.
We ask this through Christ our Lord.

or:
God of peace,
as the waters of the flood receded
you placed your bow in the clouds
to promise that you would never destroy the earth again.
Let that promise bind us also,
that we may act with justice and tenderness

to this earth and to all living beings
which you have placed in our care.
We ask this through Jesus Christ our Lord.

Proper 5: Genesis 12:1–9

The calling of Abram
God and Father of all believers,
you promised Abraham
that his descendants
would be as many as the stars of heaven,
and through the dying and rising of Christ
you have fulfilled that promise.
Everywhere throughout the world
you increase the number of your people.
Let us respond to your call
by joyfully accepting your invitation
to share the new life of grace.
This we ask through Jesus Christ our Lord.

or:
God of our pilgrimage,
you summoned Abram
to follow you in ways he did not know
and put his faith in things he could not see.
Bless all who honour him as their ancestor
and draw them together in understanding
and reverence for your name.
We ask this through Christ our Lord.

Proper 6: Genesis 18:1–15; (21:1–7)

The promise of Isaac
The prayer for Proper 5 may be repeated.

Proper 7: Genesis 21:8–21

The expulsion of Hagar
Faithful God,
whose grace, unsought and undeserved,
has made us children of your promise;
let us truly live as free men and women
in the freedom you have given us,
and, as you have delivered us from slavery to sin,
so make us labour to extend that same liberty
throughout all the earth.
We ask this through Jesus Christ our Lord.

Proper 8: Genesis 22:1–14

The sacrifice of Isaac
O God, you led your servant Abraham to the high place
where you bade him sacrifice his beloved son.
On that mountain of insight you showed him
that you desire obedience, not violence,
and that you ask of us a world
governed not by force but by compassion.
Train us in the way of this gospel,
that our worship may be true and our trust in you complete,
through your Son, Jesus Christ.

or:
Fearful God,
you require of our love
appalling sacrifice;
and your lasting promise
is contained in contradiction.
May we so lay on your altar
our deepest desires
that we may receive them back from you
as unaccountable gift,
through Jesus Christ.

Proper 9: Genesis 24:34–38, 42–49, 58–67

The finding of Rebekah
Gracious and eternal God,
you created us male and female in your image
and you brought Isaac and Rebekah together
in a bond of mutual commitment and love.
Let all our common life be ordered
on the foundations of charity,
reconciliation and peace,
that we may come to know you,
the threefold source of unity,
through Jesus Christ our Lord.

Proper 10: Genesis 25:19–34

The birth of Jacob and Esau; Esau cedes his birthright
The prayer from Proper 5 may be used.

Proper 11: Genesis 28:10–19a

Jacob's Dream
God of salvation,
whose will it is
that your rule be established on earth
and that earth be transformed
by your Spirit from on high;
hallow the places where we worship
or seek to do your good works,
so that these may be for us
the house of God and gate of heaven.
We ask this through Jesus Christ our Lord.

Proper 12: Genesis 29:15–28

Jacob succeeds in marrying Rachel
The prayer for Proper 9 may be used.

Proper 13: Genesis 32:22–31

Jacob and the stranger
The prayer from Proper 24, Year C, may be used.

or:
O God, with whom we wrestle
until the break of day,
make us long to seek your face
beyond the limits of our strength;
that in our wounds we may remember you,
and in your blessing
we may find ourselves,
through Jesus Christ.

Proper 14: Genesis 37:1–4, 12–28

Joseph is sold by his brothers
Eternal God,
whose providence is mysterious,
you sent Joseph as a slave into Egypt
that you might preserve
a remnant of his people on the earth.
Make us trust your hidden ways,
so that even in darkness
we may learn to await in hope
the light and life you will bring forth.
We ask this through Jesus Christ our Lord.

Proper 15: Genesis 45:1–15

Joseph makes himself known to his brothers
The prayer from Proper 14 may be repeated.

Proper 16: Exodus 1:8—2:10

The new regime in Egypt; the birth of Moses
The prayer from Proper 25 may be used.

Proper 17: Exodus 3:1–15

The burning bush and the Name of God
God, whose holy name
defies our definition,
but whose will is known
in freeing the oppressed,
make us to be one
with all who cry for justice;
that we who speak your praise
may struggle for your truth,
through Jesus Christ.

Proper 18: Exodus 12:1–14

Instructions for the Passover
God of our ancestors,
who commanded your people in Egypt
to eat the lamb of Passover
and to experience your salvation;
deliver us from all that oppresses the human spirit,
so that through the blood of Christ,
the Lamb who takes away our sins,
we may eat the new Passover bread
of sincerity and truth.
We ask this through Jesus Christ our Lord.

Proper 19: Exodus 14:19–31

The crossing of the Red Sea
God of wonders,
whose right hand parted the waters of the sea
and saved your people from their oppressor;
unlock for us the meaning of this marvel,
so that we,
who through baptism have been set free in Christ,
may proclaim to everyone
your word of freedom and life.
We ask this through Jesus Christ our Lord.

Proper 20: Exodus 16:2–15

Food in the desert
God of life and plenty,
you fed your people
throughout their wanderings in the desert
with manna which they had not known.
Satisfy our hungers
with the living bread of your word,
so that in the strength of this food
we may make our way
to the place of rest you have prepared for us
We ask this through Jesus Christ our Lord.

Proper 21: Exodus 17:1–7

They put the Lord to the test
Patient and merciful God,
from the hard rock
you struck living water
to quench the thirst of your people.
Unseal for us the fountain of your Spirit,
and let the faith you have bestowed
well up in us as the spring of eternal life.
This we ask through Christ our Lord.

Proper 22: Exodus 20:1–4, 7–9, 12–20

The Ten Commandments
Write upon our hearts, O God,
what once you wrote on tablets of stone
for your holy people;
so that by your Holy Spirit
we may know your law
inscribed within us,
and in our thoughts and actions
we may keep and reverence the same.
We ask this through Jesus Christ our Lord.

Proper 23: Exodus 32:1–14

Moses pleads for the people, who have worshipped the Golden Calf

God of tenderness,
recall your lasting love;
remember us and not our faults,
save us from the folly of our ways
and let your great compassion shield us
from the punishment we bring upon ourselves.
We ask this through Jesus Christ our Lord.

Proper 24: Exodus 33:12–23

Moses in the cleft of the rock

O God,
whose beauty is beyond our imagining
and whose power we cannot comprehend;
show us your glory
as far as we can grasp it,
and shield us
from knowing more than we can bear
until we may look upon you without fear,
through Jesus Christ.

Proper 25: Deuteronomy 34:1–12

The death of Moses

God of liberation,
you raised up Moses, whose memory is blessed,
to lead a people out of slavery
and teach them your holy law.
In Christ you have renewed that law for us
through the commandment of love
and the example of service.
Let us, by our obedience,
now glorify and bless your holy name.
We ask this through Jesus Christ our Lord.

Year B

The continuous reading in Year B is taken from Samuel, Kings and the Wisdom Books, including Job. The narrative begins with the call of Samuel, and covers the lives of Samuel, Saul and David. The nature of the narrative made it more difficult to find suitable collects than for Year A. The selection is, therefore, somewhat less focused than that of Year A.

Proper 4: 1 Samuel 3:1–10, (11–20)

The call of Samuel and the death of Eli
From our earliest years, O God,
you call us by our name.
Make us wise to recognize your voice,
attentive to listen and eager to respond,
that, having heard your calling
in the words of Jesus, your anointed One,
we may draw many to be his disciples.
We ask this through Jesus Christ our Lord.

Proper 5: 1 Samuel 8:4–11, (12–15,) 16–20; (11:14–15)

Samuel chooses Saul as King
God,
giver of life and source of all blessings,
let your righteousness be given
to all who lead nations,
that they may serve your people with justice,
protect them from violence,
and shield them from hardship and exploitation.
We ask this in the name of Jesus Christ, the Lord.

Proper 6: 1 Samuel 15:34–16:3

Samuel anoints David
God of insight,
you see and judge,

not according to outward appearance,
but according to the heart.
Open the eyes of our spirit,
as you opened those of Samuel your prophet,
and bestow on us the gift
of discerning your presence and purpose among us.
We ask this through Jesus Christ our Lord.

or:
O God,
you set David apart from his people
and endowed him with wisdom and strength,
so that in all things
he might glorify you, the Most High.
Keep your people steadfast
in the covenant you have made with us
and make our common life beautiful
with the songs of your praise
and the works of your justice.
We ask this through Jesus Christ our Lord.

Proper 7: 1 Samuel 17: (1a, 4–11, 19–23,) 32–49

David kills Goliath
God our security,
who alone can defend us
against the principalities and powers
that rule this present age;
may we trust in no weapons
except the whole armour of faith,
that in dying we may live,
and having nothing,
we may own the world,
through Jesus Christ.

Proper 8: 2 Samuel 1:1, 17–27

David laments the death of Saul and Jonathan
Heavenly Father,
death is not of your making,
and you have made us, not to be lost,
but to live with you for ever.
Without you, we have nothing to hope for:
with you, we have nothing to fear.
Speak to us your words of eternal life
and lift our hearts in time of grief
to the light and peace of your presence.
We ask this through Jesus Christ our Lord.

Proper 9: 2 Samuel 5:1–5, 9–10

David is fully King
The second prayer from Proper 6 may be used.

Proper 10: 2 Samuel 6:1–5, 12b–19

David brings the Ark to Jerusalem
The second prayer from Proper 6 may be used.

Proper 11: 2 Samuel 7:1–14a

Nathan promises that David will have a house of royal descendants
Faithful God,
you promised to David your servant
a royal house with heirs to rule your people,
and in the coming of Jesus, your Son,
you have brought that promise to fulfilment.
Let all on earth listen to his teaching,
so that your rule may be established
and your purposes fulfilled.
We ask this through Jesus Christ our Lord.

Proper 12: 2 Samuel 11:1–15

David's adultery with Bathsheba and his murder of Uriah
Have mercy, tender God:
for the evil we have done
stares us in the face.
We beg you, forget our defiance
and forgive our wrongdoing,
that we may acknowledge our faults
and in the confession of our misdeeds
may know your pardon and your peace.
We ask this through Jesus Christ our Lord.

Proper 13: 2 Samuel 11:26—12:13a

David is accused of sin by Nathan, and repents
Almighty and most gentle God,
who gave to your servant David
the courage to acknowledge his misdeeds;
draw forth from our hearts
the tears of true repentance,
that we may be able to lament our sins
and by your mercy
receive their forgiveness.
Through Jesus Christ our Lord

Proper 14: 2 Samuel 18:5–9, 15, 31–33

The death of Absalom and David's grief
The second prayer from Proper 6, or the prayer from Proper 8, may be used.

Proper 15: 1 Kings 2:10–12; 3:3–14

The death of David; Solomon's prayer for wisdom
God of our ancestors, source of all mercy,
by your word you formed the heavens,
and by wisdom you created humankind.

Let that wisdom labour with us
and with all who believe,
that we may know what is right
according to your commandments,
and be guided wisely
in ways that are pleasing to you.
We ask this through Jesus Christ our Lord.

Proper 16: 1 Kings 8:(1–6,10–11,) 22–30, 41–43

Solomon's prayer at the dedication of the Temple
God, whom highest heaven cannot contain,
hear the prayer of your people
and visit us with your salvation.
Guided by your word and the gift of your grace,
may your pilgrim people
now scattered over the face of the earth,
come safely to the eternal Jerusalem,
where the Lamb, your Only-Begotten,
will be for them both light and temple.
We ask this through Jesus Christ our Lord.

Proper 17: Song of Songs 2:8–13

A part of the Song of Solomon
God, our lover,
whose tender desire for us
is the very source of our being;
let us discover in your embrace
a passion for life, a delight in justice,
and the consummation of peace.
We ask this through Jesus Christ our Lord.

Proper 18: Proverbs 22:1–2, 8–9, 22–23

Some proverbs of Solomon
God of wholeness,
you have created us bodily
that our work and faith may be one.
May we offer our worship
from lives of integrity;
and maintain the fabric of this world
with hearts that are set on you,
through Jesus Christ.

or:
God, maker of us all,
you champion the cause of the poor,
and protect the life of the oppressed.
In you we have one common origin,
so may we honour you, our Creator,
by sowing the seeds of justice
and being generous helpers of the needy.
We ask this through Jesus Christ our Lord.

Proper 19: Proverbs 1:20–33

Some proverbs of Solomon: wisdom and fools
God,
you have taught us that it profits nothing
to have gained the whole world
if we have lost our soul.
Rid us of the desire
to gain possessions and power over others
and turn our hearts to you,
for in you alone we shall find true riches.
We ask this through Jesus Christ our Lord.

Proper 20: Wisdom 1:16–2:1, 12–22 (or Jeremiah 11:18–20)

Wisdom: the wicked plot against the just
Gracious Father,
whose Son by falsehood was accused,
by violence, tortured
and by hatred, killed;
watch over your people
and guard them in the way of truth,
that in Christ and in the strength of his risen life
they may overcome the world.
We ask this through Jesus Christ our Lord.

Proper 21: Esther 7:1–6, 9–10; 9:20–22

Esther reveals Haman's plot to Ahasuerus
God of justice,
remember all those who cry out to you
as their only hope of deliverance.
Do not let them be lost
but give them courage amidst their afflictions,
grace to pray for their persecutors,
and after their struggle, the vision of your glory.
We ask this through Jesus Christ our Lord.

Proper 22: Job 1:1; 2:1–10

Job's sufferings
In the depths of our isolation
we cry out to you, Lord God.
Give light in our darkness
and deliver us from despair,
so that, no matter what befalls us,
we may have the courage
to bless your holy name.
We ask this through Jesus Christ our Lord.

Proper 23: Job 23:1–9, 16–17

Job's complaint
God,
whose absence is too terrible
for us to bear,
grant that, even in abandonment,
we may recall your deeds of liberation
and that in telling of them
we may find that you are present
beyond all our expectation and fear.
We ask this through Jesus Christ our Lord.

Proper 24: Job 38:1–7, (34–41)

God's answer to Job
Glorious God,
the whole of creation proclaims your marvellous work:
increase in us the capacity to wonder and delight in it,
that heaven's praise may echo in our hearts
and our lives be spent as good stewards of your earth,
through Jesus Christ our Lord.

Proper 25: Job 42:1–6, 10–17

Job's response to God
You can do all things, O God,
and what you purpose, none can undo.
By your Spirit, increase in us
the gift of reverence and awe in your presence,
so that we may worship you in humility of heart,
and learn to place all our hope in you.
We ask this through Jesus Christ our Lord.

Year C

The continuous reading for Year C follows the tradition of the Hebrew Prophets from Elijah onwards, until the fall of Jerusalem and the exile of the people.

Proper 4: 1 Kings 18:20–21, (22–29,) 30–39

Elijah and the prophets of Baal
God of justice,
you raised up Elijah the prophet,
with words like fire
to restore your covenant among the people.
Restore to us that integrity
which you demand from those who serve you,
and turn our hearts again
towards you, our truth and our salvation.
We ask this through Jesus Christ our Lord.

Proper 5: 1 Kings 17:8–16, (17–24)

Elijah and the widow of Zarephath; he brings her son back from the dead
God, our provider,
you are the hope of the orphan,
the bread for all who are in need.
Strengthen us in faith,
that with simplicity and singleness of heart
we may trust in you alone
and serve you with wholehearted love.
We ask this through Jesus Christ our Lord.

Proper 6: 1 Kings 21:1–10, (11–14,) 15–21a

Elijah, Ahab and the vineyard of Naboth
The prayer from Proper 4 may be used.

Proper 7: 1 Kings 19:1–4, (5–7,) 8–15a
Elijah pursued by Jezebel; the still small voice
O God, from whom we flee,
whose stillness is more terrible
than earthquake, wind or fire,
speak to our loneliness
and challenge our despair;
that in your very absence
we may recognize your voice
and wrapped in your presence
we may go forth to encounter the world,
in the name of Christ.

Proper 8: 2 Kings 1:1–2, 6–14

The assumption of Elijah into heaven
The prayer from Proper 4 may be used.

Proper 9: 2 Kings 5:1–14

Elisha heals Naaman the Aramaean
O God, our life and health,
you alone are the One who saves.
Stir up in us new faith in your promises,
that, trusting in you,
we may find healing,
and render to you our thanks and praise.
We ask this through Jesus Christ the Lord.

Proper 10: Amos 7:7–17

Amos accused of treason by Amaziah
God of justice, God of salvation,
from every land you call prophets
to make known your will
and announce your judgement.
Keep them faithful to your word

and unafraid in the face of opposition,
and open the hearts of all to your gracious purpose.
We ask this through Jesus Christ our Lord.

Proper 11: Amos 8:1–12

The prophecy of famine of the word of God
Not by what we say, God of justice,
but by how we treat one another,
do you decide if our worship is acceptable,
our service pleasing in your sight.
Save us from the corruption of riches,
free our hands to assist the poor,
and set our heart on your kingdom alone.
We ask this through Jesus Christ our Lord.

Proper 12: Hosea 1:2–10

The call of Hosea
Living God,
there is no God but you.
Deliver us from the idols
which oppress and corrupt the human spirit;
confront our waywardness
and restore us to union with yourself.
Receive us once again as your people,
that we may acknowledge you as the only God.
We ask this through Jesus Christ our Lord.

Proper 13: Hosea 11:1–11

The mercy of God to Israel his child
God and Father,
with a heart of compassion
you come in search of your children,
to take them up in your arms
and lead them with the cords of love.

We pray you
gather your scattered people,
until heaven resounds in jubilation
for humanity made whole
and creation restored.
We ask this through Jesus Christ our Lord.

Proper 14: Isaiah 1:1, 10–20

The call to holiness and forgiveness
The prayer from Proper 13 may be used.

Proper 15: Isaiah 5:1–7

The vineyard of the Lord of Hosts
Who can they be,
God and master of the vineyard,
these tenants who have failed
to produce the fruits of your kingdom?
Break our hardened hearts,
pierce our self-righteous souls,
so that we may turn again to you,
and attend to our own fidelity
in bearing fruit for your kingdom.
We ask this through Jesus Christ our Lord.

Proper 16: Jeremiah 1:4–10

The call of Jeremiah
God of truth,
through the ministry of Jeremiah
you promised hope and renewal
to a people in fear of destruction and ruin.
In a time of turmoil
keep us listening for your word of tranquillity,
and as nations rouse themselves for battle,
arouse in us a passion to share your peace.
We ask this through Jesus Christ our Lord.

Proper 17: Jeremiah 2:4–13

The sins of the house of Jacob
God, the fountain of life,
let your living streams refresh our hearts
with the memory of your salvation,
so that, when we are tempted to forget you,
your word may prompt us to remember
the blessings you have showered upon us.
We ask this through Jesus Christ our Lord.

Proper 18: Jeremiah 18:1–11

The all-powerful God; prophecy of evil against Jerusalem
The prayer from Proper 16 may be used.

Proper 19: Jeremiah 4:11–12, 22–28

The foolishness of the people; a vision of universal desolation
Do not face us, O living God,
with the prospect of a wasted world
or a future of ruins and desolation;
but in your mercy,
restore to us justice,
and in your justice,
remember your overflowing mercy.
We ask this through Jesus Christ our Lord.

Proper 20: Jeremiah 8:18—9:1

A lament for Jerusalem
O God,
in your people's abandonment
you poured forth tears of sorrow
and you, the good physician
came forth with balm to heal their wounds.
Let your compassion hasten to meet us,

and for the glory of your name
deliver us, and wipe away our sins.
We ask this through Jesus Christ our Lord.

Proper 21: Jeremiah 32:1–3a, 6–15

The sale of the field at Anathoth; God promises restoration
God of all trust,
may we who confess your faith
prove it in our lives,
with abundant joy,
outrageous hope
and dependence on nothing
but your word alone,
through Jesus Christ.

Proper 22: Lamentations 1:1–6

The desolation of daughter Zion
God our Father,
you know our thoughts and share our sorrows.
Lead us out of desolation
to the caring comfort of your love.
When we forget what happiness is,
renew in us fresh springs of hope.
When we feel bereft of peace,
restore our hearts, calm our fears
and console us with the promise of life eternal.
We ask this through Jesus Christ our Lord.

Proper 23: Jeremiah 29:1, 4–7

The letter of Jeremiah to the exiles
How generous is your goodness, O God,
how great is your salvation,
how faithful is your love!
Help us to trust you in time of trial,

to praise you in time of deliverance
and at all times
to rejoice before you with overflowing hearts.
We ask this through Jesus Christ our Lord.

Proper 24: Jeremiah 31:27–34

The New Covenant
O God,
you have made us for yourself
and implanted in the human heart
a longing to be one with you.
We beg you: awaken in all peoples
the thirst to know you and the desire to love you,
so that by the Spirit of Christ
all may be gathered
into the fold of your gracious rule.
We ask this through Jesus Christ our Lord.

As an alternative, the prayer from Proper 22, Year A, is suitable.

Proper 25: Joel 2:23–32

I will pour out my Spirit on all flesh
God of light and vigour undying,
look with mercy on the whole Church,
that holy mystery and sacrament,
and in your eternal providence
complete the work of our redemption.
Let the whole world see and know
that what was fallen has been raised up,
that what was old is now made new,
and that all things are being restored to wholeness
through Christ himself,
from whom they had their origin,
who is alive for ever and ever.

III. Eucharistic Prefaces for Ordinary Time

This collection of prefaces may be used during the weeks covered by the Propers 4–25. They correspond in length to the longer prefaces proposed in Common Worship.

The work of salvation

It is truly right for us to give you thanks,
to praise and bless you, here and everywhere,
God all-holy, most gracious, full of mercy.

You are the Father of a wonderful compassion
even as you are the Lord of infinite power.
In mercy you have adopted as your children
a people once destined for slavery to sin,
and to those born on earth into the certainty of dying
you have given birth from heaven into eternal life,
through Jesus Christ your Son.

Through him, therefore, with angels and saints
we glorify your holy name: Holy . . .

Eucharist, sacrament of salvation

It is truly right, our duty and our joy,
always and everywhere to give you thanks,
Lord, holy Father, almighty and eternal God.

Christ your Son has called together
one holy people from every nation under heaven,
and with love stronger than death
has embraced them as your own.
In the sacrament of Christ's Body and Blood
that work of salvation is made present
and accomplished for us in this celebration.

Therefore, with angels and saints
we exult and glorify your holy name: Holy . . .

Christ, humbled and exalted

We lift up our hearts to you,
God of holiness and compassion;
to you we offer thanks and praise
through Jesus Christ your Son.

In Christ you have made all things new
and given us all a share in his fullness.
Though he was in the form of God,
he emptied himself
and by shedding his blood on the cross
he brought peace for the whole creation.
Therefore he was exalted above all things,
being made the source of eternal salvation
for all who serve him.

And so, with all the powers of heaven,
we glorify your name
in their unceasing hymn of praise: Holy . . .

God, the praise of earth and heaven

God most holy,
it is right for us to give you thanks
through Jesus Christ our Lord.

You are the One God, eternal, living and true.
Before all time you are; and for all eternity
you dwell in light inaccessible.
Source of life, who alone are good,
you have created all things
to fill them with your blessings
and give them joy in the radiance of your light.

Countless hosts of angels stand before you,
serving you night and day;
they gaze upon your splendour
and glorify you without end.
We also join with them
to voice the praises of your universe,
in this unceasing shout of exultation: Holy . . .

Preface of the kingdom

It is truly right and just, our joy and our salvation,
to praise you, to bless you,
to give you thanks and worship,
for you are God,
together with your only-begotten Son
and the Holy Spirit.

You brought us into being out of nothing,
you raised us up when we had fallen,
you order all things without ceasing,
that heaven may be open for us
and your kingdom bestowed on us.

For all these things we give you thanks,
but particularly because you are pleased
to receive from us the sacrifice of praise,
in communion with angels and archangels
who for ever glorify your name: Holy . . .

The Lord's Day

It is truly right, our joy and our salvation,
to give you thanks, all-holy God,
through Jesus Christ your Son.

On this, the day of his resurrection,
you gather your people together
to celebrate the mystery of our redemption.

By your saving word you teach us,
and in the Supper of the Lord
you feed us with heaven's bread and cup.
By these gifts you show us who we truly are:
a people born again into a living hope,
walking in one fellowship of love
as we await in hope the return of the Saviour.

And so, with all the powers of heaven
we glorify your holy name: Holy . . .

The Lord's Day

Father, source of truth and life,
we do well to bless you and give you thanks;
for you have gathered us together in your house
to celebrate this first day of the week,
the day you have made especially your own.

Today your family gathers,
for the hearing of your word
and for Communion in the one bread and cup.
In this we celebrate
the memorial of the risen Christ,
while we look forward
to his joyful day that will never end,
when all humanity will see you face to face
and enter at last into your rest.

And so, with angels and saints,
we sing the hymn of your glory: Holy . . .

God guides his people

We lift up our hearts to you,
God of holiness and light,
because you have called us into life,

because you are always with us,
guiding our pilgrimage on earth
with the strength of your Holy Spirit.
Christ your Son has promised
that you will let none of his people be lost,
and so we make the journey of hope
from the shadows and illusions of this life
into the light of your unceasing joy.
And so, with your angels and saints,
we glorify your holy name: Holy . . .

Christ the Saviour of all

It is truly right and just, our duty and our salvation,
always and everywhere to give you thanks,
holy Father, almighty and eternal God,
through Jesus Christ our Lord.

It is in Christ that your promises are fulfilled,
shadows give way to light, the world is reborn
and humankind becomes a new creation.
By offering himself once for all upon the cross
he desired to gather your scattered children;
and, lifted up in glory, he draws all people to himself
as the firstborn among a multitude
of his brothers and sisters.

And so, with angels and saints,
we sing the joyful hymn of your praise: Holy . . .

Thanksgiving for creation and redemption

We lift our hearts to you,
and we thank you, Father all-holy,
because you are a God of people;
you are not ashamed to be called our God;
you know us all by name;

and you hold this universe in your hands.
And that is why you have created us,
for this purpose called us into life,
that we should all be made one with you
to be your people here on earth.
We thank you, Creator of all, for giving us life,
for the light of our eyes and the air we breathe,
for all you have done among us
in Jesus Christ our Lord.
Through him we praise your name,
bowing before you, adoring you and saying: Holy . . .

The work of God in Christ

We lift our hearts to you,
and we thank you, Father all-holy,
for the sake of Jesus Christ, your beloved Son,
whom you called and sent
to bring your kingdom to the poor,
redemption to all captives,
and to be for all and for ever
the likeness and embodiment
of your constant love and goodness.
Through him we praise your name,
adoring you and saying: Holy . . .

PART THREE

PROPER TEXTS FOR THE SUNDAYS BETWEEN ALL SAINTS' AND ADVENT

The time between All Saints' Day and the beginning of Advent has increasingly been recognized as a season in its own right. This arises from a combination of several factors. First, in the Lectionary, the 'tone' of the Sundays preceding Advent – Christ the King and the previous Sunday – becomes distinctly 'eschatological', focusing on the end of time, the turmoil that Scripture portrays as characteristic of that age, and the return of Christ.

Secondly, the occurrence of two commemorations, All Saints and All Souls, tends to mark this time of the year as one of special remembering of those who have gone before us. Among Roman Catholics, November is the month devoted to prayer for the departed. This seasonal 'colour' is enhanced by the fact that Remembrance Day (or the nearest Sunday) falls during this time in Europe and the United Kingdom. This sober remembrance also points to the 'Last Things' theme.

Thirdly, in the northern hemisphere this time marks the falling of the cosmological year, the harvest, autumn and the shortening of days. Traditional religions have seen this time of the year as unusually portentous. Christianity has taken over some of this cosmological reference.

It is not surprising, therefore that the Sundays of November have been seen as a 'Kingdom Season' by the *Common Worship* tradition. This has also taken on board the traditional Harvest Festival and Dedication of a Church feasts, as well as a Sunday devoted to celebrating God's great gift of the Word, in the Holy Scriptures.

Proper texts

The texts selected and created for this season have been chosen to reflect the themes outlined above.

All Saints' Day
The Sunday between 30 October and 5 November or (if this is not kept as All Saints' Sunday) on 1 November itself

The feast of All Saints originated in the churches of the East as a celebration of those who had given their lives as martyrs for Christ. It is celebrated now to honour all those, known or unknown, whose lives were exceptional examples of the Beatitudes and Christ's commandment of love. The liturgy celebrates this day as an anticipation of the new and heavenly Jerusalem.

Scripture-related opening prayers

Year A
God, lover of humankind,
from all nations, peoples and languages
you gather your saints
into one communion of earth and heaven.
Inspire your children in this present age
to seek peace and hunger for justice,
to practise mercy and purity of heart,
so that when Christ is revealed in glory
we may recognize him as the firstborn
of many sons and daughters,
your children of the age to come.
We ask this through Jesus Christ our Lord.

Year B
God of abundant life,
in the resurrection of your Son
you have broken the power of death.

We ask you, open the eyes of our faith
towards your new and eternal Jerusalem,
where tears and mourning shall be ended,
and where all who have been faithful to Christ
will share your rich feast of salvation.
We ask this through Jesus Christ our Lord.

Year C
Eternal God,
you call us into your Church,
as members of the body of Christ,
and you mark us with the Holy Spirit
as your pledge of redemption.
Let our bodily life express
what our faith draws us to believe,
so that in communion with all your saints
we may live for the praise of your glory.
We ask this through Jesus Christ our Lord.

Opening prayer

Years ABC
Lord God, pour out upon your Church
the manifold grace of the Holy Spirit,
so that, as we celebrate the risen Christ
in the fellowship of those who have suffered
and are glorified with him,
we may obtain eternal salvation,
to the praise and glory of your name.
We ask this through Jesus Christ our Lord.

Acclamations

Year A: Matthew 5:3
V/. Alleluia, Alleluia, Alleluia.
R/. Alleluia, Alleluia, Alleluia.
V/. Jesus said: 'Blessed are the poor in spirit:

for theirs is the kingdom of heaven.'
R/. Alleluia, Alleluia, Alleluia.

Year B: John 11:44
V/. The dead man Lazarus came out and Jesus said:
'Unbind him and let him go.'

Year C: Luke 6:20
V/. The Lord said: 'Blessed are you who are poor:
for yours is the kingdom of God.'

Intercession

Years ABC
God, the fountain of all holiness,
you gave many talents to your saints on earth
and now in heaven you crown them with one glory.
Let their fellowship inspire your people,
so that each of us in our vocation as Christians
may lead a life worthy of our calling.
We ask this through Jesus Christ our Lord.

Prayer over the Gifts

Years ABC
God, our host,
at whose table we are made one,
grant that like all your saints
we may run our earthly course with faith
and have eternal communion with them in your kingdom.
We ask this through Jesus Christ our Lord.

Eucharistic Preface

Years ABC
It is truly right and just, our duty and our salvation,
always and everywhere to give you thanks,
Lord, holy Father, almighty and eternal God.

Today you gather your Church
to keep the festival of your holy city,
that heavenly Jerusalem which is our mother.
Within her walls the saints, our brothers and sisters,
crown you with praise for all eternity.
Towards them we hasten with eager steps
as pilgrims who walk by faith,
rejoicing in the glory you have given
to these members of your Church
whose radiance also you display before us
to strengthen and inspire us here on earth.

And so, with angels and all saints,
we glorify your holy name and sing: Holy . . .

Prayer after Communion

Years ABC
God our provider,
you give the one bread and one cup to feed us
and one strong hope to sustain us.
Make us one with all your saints
in the fullness of Christ's body,
so that we may rise again to glory with him
who is Lord for ever and ever.

The Fourth Sunday before Advent
The Sunday between 30 October and 5 November inclusive

This proper is used if the Feast of All Saints was celebrated on 1 November and an alternative Sunday Proper is needed.

Scripture-related opening prayers

Year A
God of steadfast love,
you ask your people to wait patiently

for the fulfilment of your purposes,
even though nations are in turmoil
and ancient certainties collapse.
Keep us faithful until the end,
and since you have called us
to your own kingdom and glory,
make us live amid this changing world
in a way that befits those
whom you desire to abide for ever.
We ask this through Jesus Christ our Lord.

Year B
Your name, O God, is the One God,
whom we are to love
with one heart and soul and strength.
Fix that name as a sign upon our hearts,
and write it in our minds.
May we fulfil and keep in word and deed
the two commandments of your kingdom,
and through loving you and our neighbour
may we find ourselves at home in your presence.
We make this prayer through Jesus Christ our Lord.

Year C
God, our salvation,
you confront our greed with your generous mercy
and graciously disarm our resistance
by coming as a guest into our midst.
Wash us from all our wickedness;
lead us to seek justice
and espouse the cause of the oppressed.
Count us among your true children,
among those found now in Christ,
who came to seek and save the lost,
who is alive and glorious for ever and ever.

Opening prayer

Years ABC
God, whose brightness shines
in the darkest places of this broken world,
open our eyes to perceive your light,
our minds to understand your truth
and our hearts to thirst for you
in whom is our complete fulfilment.
We ask this through Jesus Christ our Lord.

Acclamations

Year A: Matthew 24:14
V/. 'This good news of the kingdom must be proclaimed throughout the world:
as a testimony to the nations,' says the Lord.

Year B: Mark 12:31–3
V/. To love God and to love one's neighbour as oneself:
is more important than whole burnt offerings and sacrifices.

Year C: Luke 19:9, 10
V/. Jesus said: 'Today salvation has come to this house:
for the Son of Man came to seek out and save the lost.'

Intercession

Years ABC
Remember your Church, O God;
do not let your people forget
your call to serve the world you have created,
but make and keep us faithful to that calling.
We ask this through Jesus Christ our Lord.

Prayer over the Gifts

Years ABC
As a mother gathers her family,
so do you, our God, gather us about your table.
Make this gathering a place of welcome to the stranger,
of challenge for the strong and support for the weak,
that our communion may be truly that of Christ,
who is alive for ever and ever.

Eucharistic Preface

Years ABC
It is truly right and just, our duty and our salvation,
always and everywhere to give you thanks,
Father most holy, God of all the ages.

In you we live and move and have our being;
each day we encounter the signs of your tender care.
In the life of this mortal body
we receive even now the pledges of immortality.
Possessing the first fruits of the Spirit
who raised Jesus from the dead,
we have the sure hope
that the mystery of his dying and rising
will be for us also an eternal Easter.

Therefore with angels and all the saints
we exult and glorify your holy name: Holy . . .

Prayer after Communion

Years ABC
Gracious God,
in this present age
you admit us to the communion of the age to come.
Let this celebration send us out
as heralds of your gospel and your peace.
We ask this through Jesus Christ our Lord.

The Third Sunday before Advent
The Sunday between 6 and 12 November inclusive

Scripture-related opening prayer

Year A
Your wisdom, O God, bright and unfading,
comes quickly to those who desire you,
yet we know not the day nor the hour of her coming.
In baptism, you gave us light;
keep that light undimmed
and shining in works of justice and love,
so that on your great day
we may be worthy to enter the wedding feast
where you are the fulfilment of all desire,
for ever and ever.

Year B
God of steadfast love,
you have announced the coming of your reign
in the words and deeds of Christ your Son.
Keep your Church faithful to his call
to repentance and faith,
that your word of forgiveness
may be clearly spoken,
and the hearts of many
may be turned to you.
We ask this through Jesus Christ our Lord.

Year C
God of Abraham, Isaac and Jacob,
in your sight all are alive,
and all stand subject to your grace and judgement.
Keep us firm in the faith of Christ
and eager for the coming of your reign,
that your good hope may strengthen us
as we await the resurrection to eternal life

and the glory of our Lord Jesus Christ,
who is with you and the Holy Spirit,
one living and true God for ever and ever.

Opening prayer

Years ABC
Eternal God,
you call your people
to walk as pilgrims in this passing world
with eyes set on your holy city.
Go before us on our journey,
show us the way of holiness
and bring us to our journey's end in peace.
We ask this through Jesus Christ our Lord.

Acclamations

Year A: Matthew 25:13
V/. 'Keep awake, therefore,' says the Lord:
'for you know neither the day nor the hour.'

Year B: Mark 1:15
V/. Jesus said, 'The kingdom of God has come near:
repent and believe in the good news.'

Year C: Luke 20:38
V/. The Lord said: 'God is God of the living:
for to him all are alive.'

Intercession

Years ABC
Gracious God,
you gather a people as your own,
not to remove them from the world
but to make them shine as this world's light.

Fill your Church with the gifts of the Spirit,
and make us effective witnesses to Jesus,
that all the earth may echo
the unceasing song of your praise.
We ask this through Jesus Christ our Lord.

Prayer over the Gifts

Years ABC
Gracious God,
whose word is the true food,
give us words to thank you for your gifts,
and lives that will be a blessing for others.
We ask this through Jesus Christ our Lord.

Eucharistic Preface

Years ABC
It is truly right and just, our duty and our salvation,
always and everywhere to give you thanks,
Lord, holy Father, almighty and eternal God.

You have established our human destiny,
that we should be born into this present world
to receive the gift of eternal life in your kingdom.
By the power of your word you fashioned us from earth
so that in tender love you might fill us
with the abundance of your heavenly gifts.

And so, with angels and saints,
we exult and glorify your holy name: Holy . . .

Prayer after Communion

Years ABC
In this Communion, O God,
we have tasted the bread of your presence
and the wine of the age to come.

Keep our hearts fixed on you
and on the inheritance of glory
that is promised to those who are faithful.
We ask this through Christ our Lord.

The Second Sunday before Advent
The Sunday between 13 and 19 November inclusive

Scripture-related opening prayers

Year A
God of nature, God of grace,
you entrust to our hands
many skills and talents
to be used and perfected in your service.
Let us not be afraid to employ what you have given,
and multiply our good works from the resources you bestow,
so that at the last, you may find us faithful
and summon us to share your joy.
We ask this through Jesus Christ our Lord.

Year B
You promise, O God,
not to abandon us to death,
but to deliver us on the day of ruin.
In these last times,
equip us with the spirit of right judgement
that we may not follow false prophets
nor be alarmed amid rumours of war;
but strengthen us to endure the labours
which will herald the birth of your new age.
We ask this through Jesus Christ our Lord.

Year C
God our Saviour,
you bid us face these last days, not with fear,
but by doing what is right.

When there is tumult and turmoil,
show us the favourable time
to testify to your gospel,
and when we are called to speak,
give us your words and wisdom.
Then, when the Sun of Righteousness dawns
let him find us steadfast
and reward us with life eternal.
For he is the living One, now and for ever.

Opening prayer

Years ABC
God of steadfast love,
be moved, we pray you,
by the fragility of our mortal nature,
and let the prayer of faith
be heard in your merciful presence;
so that although we have nothing of our own
to justify us before you,
your abundant mercy may give us everything.
This we ask through Jesus Christ, our Lord.

Acclamations

Year A: Matthew 25:21
V/. 'Well done, good and trustworthy slave:
enter into the joy of your master.'

Year B: Mark 13:7
V/. Jesus said, 'When you hear of wars and rumours of wars, do not be alarmed:
this must take place, but the end is still to come.'

Year C: Luke 21:15
V/. 'I will give you words and a wisdom,' says the Lord:
'that none of your opponents will be able to contradict.'

Intercession

Years ABC
God of wisdom,
you know everything we ask or desire.
Inspire, we pray you, our thoughts and speech
to ask those things that will be for your glory
and for the salvation of the whole world.
We make this prayer through Jesus Christ our Lord.

Prayer over the Gifts

Years ABC
Bless, Lord, our worship at your table,
and grant that as your Church was born
from the pierced side of Christ on the cross,
so we may always draw holiness
from communion with his risen life.
Through Christ our Lord.

Eucharistic Preface

Years ABC
It is truly right and just, our duty and our salvation,
always and everywhere to give you thanks,
Lord, holy Father, almighty and eternal God,
through Jesus Christ our Lord.

As the Word made flesh
he came to live in lowly form amongst us.
As the immortal One, he assumed this mortal body
to suffer on the cross and be laid in the tomb.
But with great power he rose from the dead
so that he might raise us together with himself
and clothe our corruptible nature
with an incorruptible and eternal life.

And so, with angels and all saints,
we exult and glorify your holy name: Holy . . .

Prayer after Communion

Generous God,
may we accept your kingdom
like children taking bread
from their father's hand.
Like infants at their mother's breast
may we drink of your Spirit
and live and share your peace always.
We ask this through Jesus Christ our Lord.

Christ the King – The Sunday next before Advent
The Sunday between 20 and 26 November inclusive

This feast was instituted in the Roman Catholic Church in 1925, to celebrate Christ's universal kingdom. In the liturgical reforms of 1969 it was transferred to the last Sunday before Advent, in keeping with the eschatological nature of these Sundays. We celebrate Christ as the sign of contradiction: the crucified King, the Holy One who is rejected, the Judge who is arraigned before a human tribunal, whose dying and rising inaugurate the new age of God's rule.

Scripture-related opening prayers

Year A
God, whose coming judgement
will shake the earth and heaven,
just as in the advent of Christ
you overturned all images of earthly power;
prepare us for that awesome day
when the Son of Man will appear in glory.
Shape our lives according to his teaching
that what we do for the least of his brothers and sisters
we shall have done for him,
the Christ who is, and was, and is to come,
who is alive, and reigns for ever and ever.

Year B
God, whose kingdom is not of this world
yet whose rule governs everything within it,
you have called us in Christ
to be a kingdom and a priestly people.
Make us both learn and practise
this new kingship of Christ
by testifying to your truth
and serving others in your love.
For yours is true glory and power
for ever and ever.

Year C
From a cross, O God,
your Christ, the firstborn of creation,
has taken up his rule.
Fashion our lives after the pattern of this cross,
school our hearts in his compassion,
and since he has brought us to share
in the inheritance of the saints in light,
lead us by his shepherd's hand
into the fold of eternal life in paradise.
We ask this through Jesus Christ our Lord.

Opening prayer

Years ABC
Christ, light of the world,
whose death shattered the bonds of death,
grant that all who are imprisoned
in the darkness of tyranny and oppression
may find in you the light of true freedom,
and enter into the joy of your eternal rule.
For with the Father and the Holy Spirit
you are one in glory, for ever and ever.

Acclamations

Year A: Matthew 25:40
V/. The King will answer, 'As you did this to the least among my family:
you did it to me.'

Year B: John 18:37
V/. Jesus said, 'For this I was born and for this I came into the world:
to testify to the truth.'

Year C: Luke 23:43
V/. 'Truly I tell you,' said the Lord:
'today you will be with me in paradise.'

Intercession

Year ABC
Confirm, O God, the work you have done in us,
and preserve in the hearts of your people
the gifts of the Holy Spirit,
that they may not be ashamed
to acknowledge Christ crucified,
but may carry out his commandments
with unfailing love.
This we ask through Jesus Christ our Lord.

Prayer over the Gifts

Years ABC
Eternal God,
as we celebrate the sacrifice of Christ
which has reconciled all things to you,
we pray that your Son will bestow upon the world
the gifts of unity and peace,
for he is alive and reigns for ever and ever.

Eucharistic Preface

Years ABC
We lift up our hearts to you,
God of holiness and wisdom;
to you we offer thanks and praise
through Jesus Christ your Son.

Though he is one with you in glory
he emptied himself to share our human nature,
so that by accepting our mortal suffering
he might restore us to fellowship with you.
Now, as the risen One,
he has poured out upon the Church
the promised gift of the Holy Spirit,
making us partakers in what belongs to him,
the ministry of priest, prophet and king.

And so, with angels and all saints
we exult and glorify your holy name: Holy . . .

Prayer after Communion

Years ABC
Eternal God,
by this holy feast
you make us one with Christ.
Keep us in that holy fellowship
that we may perform those good works
which you have prepared for us to do.
We ask this through Jesus Christ our Lord.

Harvest Thanksgiving

The Harvest Festival originated in nineteenth-century Anglicanism and has become hugely popular. It focuses not just on the ingathering of the fruits of the land, but also on Christ, the 'first fruits of those who have died' (cf. 1 Corinthians 15:20)*. Its* *position at this stage in the year gives it an eschatological flavour, as is found in many of the great harvest hymns.*

Scripture-related opening prayers

Year A
God, the source of all good things,
from the fruit of the earth, your bountiful gift,
you satisfy the needs of every living creature.
Keep us mindful of your generous mercy
and faithful in keeping your commandments,
that all may share justly in what you have bestowed,
and come in thanksgiving to bless your holy name.
We make this prayer through Jesus Christ our Lord.

Year B
God of abundance,
you give the sun and rain
and make the earth fruitful.
Remove from our human community
the fear of want and the menace of starvation.
Make us generous in giving,
and wise in our husbandry of this good earth,
that all may eat and praise your holy name.
We ask this through Jesus Christ our Lord.

Year C
God of salvation,
you rejoice with your people
in the harvest of what you have provided.
Give us the true bread of life
in the gospel of our Lord Jesus Christ,
and make us one body in that one living bread,
so that by the power of the Holy Spirit
your Church may gather
a harvest of faith from every tongue and nation.
We ask this through Jesus Christ our Lord.

Opening prayer

Years ABC
We give you thanks, O God,
for the harvest which earth has produced for our good;
and we pray
that as your providence has given these fruits of the soil,
so by your gift
may the seeds of charity and justice
bear fruit in our hearts.
We make this prayer through Jesus Christ our Lord.

Acclamations

Year A: Luke 12:21
V/. Let us not store up treasures for ourselves:
but be rich in the sight of God.

Year B: Matthew 6:33
V/. 'Strive first for the kingdom of God and his righteousness:
and all these things will be given to you as well,' says the Lord.

Year C: John 6:35
V/. Jesus said to them, 'I am the bread of life:
whoever comes to me shall not be hungry.'

Intercession

Years ABC
Father of all that is good,
whose providence has entrusted the earth to humankind,
grant that, using what the earth has yielded us,
we may be able to support the life of all,
so that the fulfilment of their needs
may redound to your glory.
Through Christ our Lord.

Prayer over the Gifts

Years ABC
Gracious God,
as we place upon your table
the fruits of earth and human labour,
we ask that you will make us fruitful
in the works of love that you hold out to us.
We ask this through Jesus Christ our Lord.

Eucharistic Preface

Years ABC
It is truly right and just, our duty and our salvation,
always and everywhere to give you thanks,
Lord, holy Father, almighty and eternal God.

You are the maker of all things,
you have decreed the changing of times and seasons.
You fashioned the human race in your likeness
and entrusted to them the care of your wonderful works,
that we might set forward your purpose for creation
and praise you for the wonderful work of your hands
through Jesus Christ our Lord.

Through him, therefore, with angels and all saints,
we exult and glorify your holy name: Holy . . .

Prayer after Communion

Years ABC
God our provider,
from the fruit of the earth
you feed us with the bread of heaven.
Make us faithful stewards of your gifts
and grant, even now, a foretaste of that glory
with which you will clothe the whole of creation.
We ask this through Jesus Christ our Lord.

Bible Sunday
May be celebrated in preference to the provision for the last Sunday after Trinity

In the Book of Common Prayer, *the Collect for the Second Sunday of Advent (a text based on the New Testament reading for that Sunday from Saint Paul's Letter to the Romans) celebrates the great gift of God to us, God's Word in Holy Scripture. In many churches, that day came to be celebrated as 'Bible Sunday'. Given the importance of the Advent Season, this commemoration may now be celebrated on the Last Sunday after Trinity.*

Scripture-related opening prayers

Year A
God, Creator and Saviour,
yours is the word by which all things came to be,
the word of liberation in Law and prophets,
and finally, the Word made Flesh in Jesus your Son.
Let Christ abide in us;
touch our senses, enlighten our minds
and let your Spirit transform us into a people
who do everything in his name,
their lives a song of blessing and praise.
We make this prayer through Jesus Christ our Lord.

Year B
Transcendent God,
your word has gone forth
to accomplish your purpose of salvation.
Grant to us a spirit of discernment and faith,
and as we hear, read and contemplate the holy Scriptures
lead us to discern therein
the presence and work of Christ,
and to know him, who is our eternal life.
We ask this in his name,
who is alive, and reigns for ever and ever.

Year C
O God, whose word goes forth in righteousness,
you desire that all should be saved
and come to know your truth.
Let that word be on the lips
and in the heart of all your people,
so that by the power of your Holy Spirit
the world may hear your gospel of liberation,
and through it come to know you, the One true God,
and Jesus, the Christ whom you have sent,
who is alive, and reigns with you for ever and ever.

Opening prayer

Years ABC
Holy Spirit of God,
rest upon this assembly
in its hearing of the Scriptures,
in its reflection upon their words
and in its discipleship of Christ,
that every knee may bow before his name,
who lives and reigns for ever and ever.

Acclamations

Year A: Matthew 24:35
V/. Jesus says: 'Heaven and earth shall pass away:
but my words will not pass away.'

Year B: John 5:36
V/. Jesus said, 'The works that the Father has given me:
these very works testify that the Father has sent me.'

Year C: Luke 4:22
V/. All spoke well of him and were amazed:
at the gracious words that came from his mouth.

Intercession

Years ABC
Lord, grant your people grace and protection:
give them health of mind and body,
that they may abide in your word,
live in love and charity with their neighbours
and remain always faithful to you.
We ask this through Jesus Christ our Lord.

Prayer over the Gifts

Years ABC
O God, whose word has gathered us
around this table of thanksgiving,
Let the Communion which you offer us here
unite our lives to yours.
We ask this through Jesus Christ our Lord.

Eucharistic Preface

Years ABC
It is truly right and just, our duty and our salvation,
always and everywhere to give you thanks,
Lord, holy Father, almighty and eternal God.

You have made known your salvation
through your living word,
inspiring its telling and recording
by the breath of the Holy Spirit.
You desire to write it upon our hearts,
so that, like fertile seed planted within us,
it may bear fruit to your praise and glory
through Jesus Christ our Lord.

And so, with angels and all saints
we exult and glorify your holy name: Holy . . .

Prayer after Communion

Years ABC
God of love,
you have fed us at the table of your word,
where Christ is both host and food.
As your abundance has been poured out on us,
so make us attentive to the needs of others
and worthy of that heavenly banquet
which you have prepared
for those who truly love and serve you.
We ask this through Jesus Christ our Lord.

Dedication Festival
The first Sunday in October or last Sunday after Trinity

The anniversary of the dedication of a church is usually observed on the day itself. However, in many cases where the record of the actual date of dedication has been lost, it is customary to celebrate it during the month of October. The dedicated church building reminds us that it is Domus Ecclesiae, *the 'House of the Church', God's people, who are the* ecclesia, *those 'called out' of the world to serve God in Christ.*

Scripture-related opening prayers

Year A
God most high and most holy,
heaven itself cannot contain you,
yet in every generation
you build your dwelling place on earth
as the temple of your Spirit,
founded on Christ, its precious cornerstone.
Hear the prayers of your Church,
gathered in this house
to celebrate its dedication to your service.

Make this community a true house of prayer,
a place of praise to your holy name.
We make this prayer through Jesus Christ our Lord.

Year B
God of salvation,
who revealed to our ancestor Jacob
the house of God and gate of heaven,
be present also in this place
whose dedication we celebrate today.
Build us, who gather here, into a spiritual house,
a people set apart for your praise and glory,
so that we, and all who have tasted your goodness,
may grow towards eternal salvation
in Christ Jesus, the cornerstone,
who is one with you and the Holy Spirit
for ever and ever.

Year B – when Revelation 21:9–14 is read in place of Genesis 28:11–18
God of salvation,
you have revealed to your people
the new and heavenly Jerusalem
as the place of your eternal dwelling.
Be present also in this place
whose dedication we celebrate today.
Build us, who gather here, into a spiritual house,
a people set apart for your praise and glory,
so that we, and all who have tasted your goodness,
may grow towards eternal salvation
in Christ Jesus, the cornerstone,
who is one with you and the Holy Spirit
for ever and ever.

Year C
All things come from you, O God,
and from your many gifts of skill and labour

this place whose dedication we recall today
was built to shelter your Church.
Speak to us here of Christ,
whose body we are called to be,
that your Church may be built on him,
as a spiritual house of prayer for all,
and a holy temple for your glory.
We ask this through Jesus Christ our Lord.

Opening prayer

Years ABC
Eternal God,
you give us again each year
the day of this church's dedication.
Hear the prayers of your people
and grant that in this place
a pure offering of service may be made to you,
and your abundant redemption extended to us.
We ask this through Jesus Christ our Lord.

Acclamations

Year A: Matthew 21:13
V/. Jesus said to them, 'It is written:
"My house shall be called a house of prayer."'

Year B: John 10:27
V/. Jesus said to them, 'My sheep hear my voice:
I know them and they follow me.'

Year C: John 2:19, 21
V/. Jesus said, 'Destroy this temple and in three days I will raise it up':
but he was speaking of the temple of his body.

Intercession

Years ABC
Father of all, we ask you,
as we celebrate the dedication of this church,
to strengthen our communion with each other
and with all your people
across the face of the earth.
We ask this through Jesus Christ our Lord.

Prayer over the Gifts

Years ABC
Mindful of the day, O God,
on which you filled your house
with glory and holiness,
we ask that you make of us
a sacrifice well-pleasing in your sight.
Grant this through Jesus Christ our Lord.

Eucharistic Preface

Years ABC
It is truly right and just, our duty and our salvation,
always and everywhere to give you thanks,
Lord, holy Father, almighty and eternal God,
through Jesus Christ our Lord.

You allow us to build this visible dwelling
where you never cease to encourage your people
on their pilgrimage towards you.
Here in sacramental signs
you manifest and accomplish
the mystery of your communion with us.
Here also you build up that temple which is ourselves,
until your Church throughout the world
is made perfect as the true body of Christ
and reaches its fullness

in the heavenly city, Jerusalem,
the vision of your peace.

And so, with angels and all saints,
we exult and glorify your holy name: Holy . . .

Prayer after Communion

Years ABC
We pray you, Lord our God,
let your dedicated people take with them
the fruits of your blessing and joy,
that the Church which we have celebrated today
may be truly revealed in our lives and actions.
We ask this through Jesus Christ our Lord.

PART FOUR

TEXTS FOR EVENING PRAYER OF SATURDAY OR A SUNDAY VIGIL SERVICE

Christians keep Sunday sacred because it is the 'Lord's Day' – the day of the resurrection of Christ. It is traditional in Anglican worship and in many other historic traditions to begin the celebration of Sunday at Evening Prayer on Saturday.

This tradition might be expressed by the solemn celebration of Saturday Evening Prayer or the celebration of a Saturday evening Vigil Service for Sunday. In this section, prayers and other material are proposed which might form part of such a service.

The Evening Prayer or Vigil might begin with a Service of Light. One of the sets of texts on pp. 185–8 for All Saints' Day or 132–5 for Candlemas might be used. Some other hymns and prayers, suitable for any Sunday, are given below.

The service might also include a rite of burning incense as a celebration of the resurrection and a prayer for forgiveness and purification. In the Byzantine Liturgy, Vespers is celebrated with the burning of incense, during which parts of Psalm 141 are sung. On Saturday evenings, when Vespers is the first service of Sunday, these psalm verses are complemented by a series of prose verses celebrating the resurrection of Christ. There are eight sets of these and they are sung over an eight-week cycle, each to one of the eight musical tones in use in the Byzantine Rite. The sets of verses given below are a free translation of parts of these prose hymns.

Groups intending to celebrate a Vigil will need to plan its 'choreography' and decide how they are to use light, incense (if desired) and even other symbols such as baptismal water (cf. the Commemoration of Baptism on pp. 177–9), how the assembly space is to be laid out, how the readings are to be presented, if audio or visual aids are to be used, and so on. Since the aim of a vigil is to listen to and reflect upon the Word of God, allowing it to sink into the heart, the space where it is celebrated and the pacing and manner of its celebration need to be carefully considered beforehand.

The Service of Light

(Common Worship – Daily Prayer *(Church House Publishing 2002) makes provision also for this on p. 84.)*

The Leader opens the service with the words:

In the name of our Lord Jesus Christ,
light and peace be with you all.

All reply:

And also with you.

Lights are kindled as required. The Easter Candle may be used. The following hymns are suitable. The first group of hymns are all versions of the ancient Greek evening hymn 'Joyful Light', a version of which is given below:

O joyful light,
from the pure glory of the eternal heavenly Father,
O holy, blessed Jesus Christ.

As we come to the setting of the sun
and see the evening light,
we give thanks and praise to the Father and to the Son
and to the Holy Spirit of God.

Worthy are you at all times
to be sung with holy voices,
O Son of God, O giver of life,
and to be glorified through all creation.

or one of these versions of the same hymn:

Hail, gladdening light (Hymns for Today's Church 275)
O gladsome light (New English Hymnal 247)
O gracious light, Lord Jesus Christ (Laudate 14)
Light of gladness (Laudate 15)

or:

O Trinity of blessed light (New English Hymnal 54)
Christ, mighty Saviour (Worship 681)
Thy strong word didst cleave the darkness (Worship 511)
'I am the light of the world,' says the Lord (Gather 510)
The Light of Christ (Gather 511)

Prayers that may be used at the Service of Light:
O Lord our God, who are the very source and origin of light! At the end of this day we, your unworthy servants, come before you with our evening praise and spiritual worship. As the light of this world fades into darkness, we give you thanks for sending us your eternal light, our Lord, Jesus Christ. In his name we implore you to enlighten our souls and bodies, that we may come to the knowledge of your truth and the faithful observance of your precepts. For you are our God and we give you glory, Father, Son and Holy Spirit, now and for ever, and unto ages of ages:
R/. Amen.

Or:

Blessed are you, Lord our God, King of the universe!
Your word brings on the dusk at evening,
your wisdom creates both night and day.

You determine the cycles of time,
arrange the succession of the seasons
and establish the stars in their heavenly courses.
Lord of the starry hosts is your name.
Living and eternal God, rule over us always.
Blessed be the Lord, whose word makes evening fall.

Rite of Incense

In this Rite, Psalm 141:2 is used as the refrain for a series of short lyrics that celebrate the resurrection of Christ. As explained above, there are eight of these. I have tried to arrange the refrain so that it might be easily sung in one of the eight musical modes used in Western Plainchant. A simple four-line psalm tone will suffice for the lyrics.

The First Set

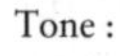

R/. Let my prayer rise like incense;
    my uplifted hands like the evening sacrifice.

O risen Lord, let this our evening prayer
Arise like fragrant incense in your sight;
You are the living One who died and rose
Revealing resurrection to the world.

Let all arise and circle Zion with joy
And glorify the One who rose from death;
The Christ, the living, true, eternal God
Who saved us from our sins by his own blood.

Let all adore the Lord and sing his praise,
and glorify the resurrection from the dead;
Christ is our Lord and God who trampled down
Our ancient and deceitful enemy.

Rejoice, O heaven! Let your trumpets sound!
Let earth's foundations shake with happy mirth!
For Christ by dying has destroyed our death,
Restoring life to Adam and his race.

To Christ who in the flesh bore death for us,
Who suffered and was buried and rose up;
We pray: 'Confirm your Church in truth and praise,
Give peace to all, O friend of humankind!'

The Second Set

R/. Let my prayer rise like incense;
my uplifted hands like the evening sacrifice.

Come, let us worship Christ the Son of God,
The First-Begotten, now of Mary born,
Who by his own free will accepted death
And rose again to save and raise the lost.

By dying, Christ has trampled over death,
Death's might is now undone, its sting is crushed;
Let us adore the risen glorious Lord,
his third-day rising praise, his glory sing.

With all creation's powers let us praise
The rising of the Lord who saves our souls;
For he will come again to judge the world
Which his creating hand has formed and made.

The women came with myrrh, the angel spoke:
'Why seek the living here among the dead?
For just as he foretold, the Lord is risen,
The source of life is risen from the tomb.'

You burst the gates of death, broke down its doors,
Then from the darkness brought your people home;
Led by your hand they came forth into light,
Singing your praise, the Lord of endless life.

The Third Set

Tone :

R/. Let my prayer rise like incense;
my uplifted hands like the evening sacrifice.

You broke the grip of death, O Christ our Saviour,
When on the cross you foiled our ancient foe;
By faith you save us and to faith you call us,
Praise be to you, Redeemer of the world!

Your rising floods the universe with glory;
The way to paradise is opened wide;
With sounds of joy the whole creation echoes,
Praise be to you, Redeemer of the world!

Down to the place of death the living Saviour
Descended to announce the gracious words:
'Take heart, for I have conquered, I am risen!
I am the resurrection and the life.'

Amid your Church, O Christ our God, we bless you
And offer you our evening hymns of praise:
O Christ the friend of humankind, the risen One,
O save us, grant us peace and raise us up!

We praise the Father, Son and Holy Spirit,
The uncreated Godhead do we praise;
True God, in essence One and Undivided,
Who reigns for ever, Trinity sublime!

The Fourth Set

Tone :

R/. Let my prayer rise like incense;
 my uplifted hands like the evening sacrifice.

Your life-bestowing cross we praise and honour,
We glorify your rising, Christ our God;
Through them you have renewed our fallen nature
And brought us back to walk your holy ways.

Upon the cross-tree you, the Judge, were seated,
The former tree's dark sentence to annul;
Descending to death's prison, you, most mighty,
shattered its doors and set its prisoners free.

By dying you destroyed our death, O Saviour;
You broke the bonds of death, O Christ our God;
You freed us from corruption by your mercy
And life immortal you have brought to all.

Come, let us sing our Saviour's resurrection,
And with the angels praise and thank the Lord;
Who brought us out of death to incorruption,
And shed his glorious light on humankind.

Your coming from the Father is eternal,
Your incarnation is beyond all power to tell;
Your advent with the dead strikes death with terror,
For now you have destroyed its pain and fear.

The Fifth Set

Tone :

R/. Let my prayer rise like incense;
my uplifted hands like the evening sacrifice.

You broke the power of death, Lord Jesus Christ,
when on the cross you offered up your life;
And by your glorious rising from the dead,
You led us forth from darkness into light.

Led to the slaughter like a spotless lamb
You are our Passover of life and peace;
You went into the darkest realm of death
to set its captives free and lead them forth.

Christ who has made all things, seen and unseen,
In love for all has suffered in the flesh;
And in the flesh is risen from the dead,
The promise of a glory yet to be.

O Light undying, hear our evening praise,
For you have filled the universe with light;
Your light divine transforms our human flesh
And shines for ever, mirrored in your saints.

Glory to you, our Saviour and our Lord,
Whose resurrection makes the angels sing,
Brings joy to Adam and all righteous souls
And opens wide the way to paradise.

The Sixth Set

Mode Six

Tone :

R/. Let my prayer rise like incense;
my uplifted hands like the evening sacrifice.

When you were lifted high upon the cross,
You raised up those who sat enchained in death,
For you alone are free of death's dominion;
O risen Saviour, source of light, have mercy!

Today the risen Lord fills earth with gladness,
Who trampled death and rose as he had said;
O Christ who dwell in light, the fount of life,
O risen Saviour, source of light, have mercy.

Where can we flee to hide ourselves from you?
Not up to heaven for there you make your dwelling;
Nor to the grave, for there you conquered death.
O risen Saviour, source of light, have mercy.

We sing our hymn of praise to you, O Christ,
Who by your death destroyed the power of death
And rising, promised glory to all flesh;
O risen Saviour, source of light, have mercy.

Lord Jesus, first-begotten from the dead,
The first fruits of God's harvesting to come,
You will return in glory as the judge;
O risen Saviour, source of light, have mercy.

The Seventh Set

Tone :

R/. Let my prayer rise like incense;
my uplifted hands like the evening sacrifice.

O come and let us sing for joy to God!
O heavenly powers, praise the risen Lord
Who broke the tyranny and rule of death;
O Maker, Saviour, glory be to you!

The cross and burial you endured for us,
You trampled death by rising for our sake;
Your third-day rising we adore and praise,
O Maker, Saviour, glory be to you!

To you, the risen One, the Apostles sang:
'You are the glory of the Church, O Christ!
You are the life and light of all who live.'
O Maker, Saviour, glory be to you!

Freely you went into the place of death,
You broke its doors and opened wide its gates;
Adam and Eve burst forth in songs of praise:
'O Maker, Saviour, glory be to you.'

As one who sleeps, O Christ, you slept in death,
From death you rose, awakening in strength;
With you the righteous also rise and sing:
'O Maker, Saviour, glory be to you!'

The Eighth Set

R/. Let my prayer rise like incense;
 my uplifted hands like the evening sacrifice.

Now as the sun goes down we worship you
In spirit and in truth, O Christ our God;
For through your resurrection from the dead
You grant us life and mercy, one and all.

Lord Jesus Christ, our Saviour and our God,
Do not abandon those whom you have called;
But through your glorious rising from the dead,
O grant us life and mercy, one and all.

Rejoice O Zion, City of our God!
God's holy dwelling, Mother of the Church!
For through the resurrection, Christ the Lord
has given you life and mercy, one and all.

The Sole-Begotten Son and Word of God,
Incarnate from the Virgin Mary's womb,
Freely accepted death upon the cross
And by his rising brought us endless life.

Glory to you, O Christ, eternal Son,
The crucified and ever-living Lord;
Receive our evening prayer of joyful praise
And save us all, O friend of humankind.

Prayer to conclude the Rite of Incense

Ever-faithful God,
you love us and bless us
in Jesus Christ your Son.
By him alone
you are perfectly glorified.
At this evening hour
may your Spirit in us
sing the marvels of your salvation;
God most high,
who live for ever and ever.

or:

We give you thanks, Lord our God,
for this day, now drawing to a close.
May our prayer, rising before you like incense,
be pleasing to you;
and may our outstretched hands
be filled with your mercy,
through Jesus, your Son, our Lord.

or:

Lord our God,
this day is drawing to a close.
At the hour of evening sacrifice
you gather us in praise.
Keep us from all anxiety
and stir up in our hearts
a longing for your day.
Hear us in the love you bear us
through Christ
and in the Holy Spirit,
for ever and ever.

If Evening Prayer is to form the rest of the service, it begins with the Word of God – the Psalmody as set out on p. 41 of Common Worship. *The readings will be those appointed in the Daily Office Lectionary.*

The Liturgy of the Word

If a Service of the Word is to be celebrated, it follows the Service of Light (and that of Incense) with the Collect and the rest as outlined on p. 24 of Common Worship.

Saturday or a Sunday Vigil Service

If the Saturday Evening Vigil is a regular part of worship, then readings may be chosen on a 'continuous reading' basis from one of the available lectionaries.

Otherwise, one option for the choice of readings might be to choose from the readings suggested in the Lectionary for the years other than that which is currently under way. The Second and Third Service options might also be used, if appropriate.

Between the readings, canticles may be used (see the selection in Common Worship – Daily Prayer *(Church House Publishing 2002) pp. 493–575), followed by times of silence. If appropriate, the Scripture-related opening prayers for the Sunday might be used after the responsorial canticle.*

A psalm or psalms may be recited before the readings, or between them as an alternative to canticles. If psalm prayers are desired, the psalms should be followed by a time of silence and the psalm prayer. Common Worship – Daily Prayer *has psalm prayers attached to the psalms in the Psalter, pp. 575ff. It is appropriate for people to sit for the psalms and prayers.*

The Taizé responses might be useful aids to prayer during the readings at the Vigil.

If non-Scripture readings are desired to follow the Scripture readings, these might be taken from Celebrating the Seasons *(Canterbury Press 1999) or another collection of spiritual readings, such as:* From the Fathers to the Churches *(Collins 1983) or* Christ our Light – Patristic Readings on Gospel Themes *(Exordium Books 1981) which follows the Roman Gospel lectionary for Sundays and so, in great part, the* Common Worship *Sunday Lectionary.*

The readings should conclude with the Gospel of the coming Sunday, preceded by the acclamation Alleluia *with appropriate verse, or a suitable hymn.*

The outline of A Service of the Word *allows for a homily, but this is not necessary if a reading from the Patristic tradition appropriate to the Gospel has been chosen.*

Long readings may be read in short portions with silence between them rather than as one single extract.

The Conclusion of the Vigil

The Vigil may end with the hymn Te Deum Laudamus, *followed by the Collect of the Sunday, a blessing and dismissal.*

PART FIVE

OTHER MATERIAL FOR THE MAIN SERVICE OF SUNDAY

In this section, texts are given that might serve as options for the opening rites of the Eucharist. Some of this material is also appropriate for main services that are not to be the Eucharist.

On the Feast of the Presentation of the Lord (Candlemas), it is traditional to begin the Eucharist with a procession of the ministers and the whole congregation. This usually takes the place of the opening rites and concludes with the Collect, after which the Ministry of the Word proceeds as usual. A form for the Candlemas Procession is given on pp. 16–17.

It might be appropriate on some other Sundays to begin the Eucharist with a commemoration of our baptism.

The Commemoration of Baptism

If the church has a prominent baptismal font near the main doors or on the main axis of the church, it should have a vessel of water placed within or alongside it and the congregation might be asked to turn to face it. Alternatively, a vessel of water might be prepared in the sanctuary or in the centre of the church.

When the ministers have entered, the president greets the people in the usual way and then says this invitation to prayer:

Dear friends in Christ,
this is the day
when Jesus passed through the deep waters of death

to risen life in the Holy Spirit.
Let us ask God to renew that same Spirit in us,
that we may live more intensely
the covenant with God which was made in our baptism.

After a brief period of silent prayer, the president recites one of the following prayers.

God our Father,
your gift of water
brings life and freshness to the earth;
in baptism it washes away our sins
and by the gift of the Holy Spirit
gives us new birth into eternal life.

We ask you now
to bless this water
and to give us your protection on this day
which you have made your own.
Renew the living spring of your life within us
and protect us in spirit and body,
that we may be free from sin
and come into your presence
to receive your gift of salvation.
We ask this through Jesus Christ our Lord.

or:

Blessed be God, Creator of the universe:
R/. Blessed be the name of the Lord.
Blessed be the Lord Jesus, the resurrection and the life:
R/. Blessed be the name of the Lord.
Blessed be the Holy Spirit, the Lord and life-giver:
R/. Blessed be the name of the Lord.

Blessed are you for this water
which reminds us of our dignity

as your baptized people,
and of your tender mercy
in calling us to share your threefold life,
Father, Son and Spirit,
for ever and ever
R/. Amen.

The President sprinkles the people with water.

(A conventional sprinkler might be used, or better, a bunch of rosemary, or sprigs of box, tied together to form a brush.)

During the sprinkling, a psalm or hymn may be sung, for instance:

Water of Life (Laudate 512)
Give us Lord, a new heart (Laudate 514)
Baptized in water (Hymns for Today's Church 381)

After the sprinkling, Glory to God in the Highest *is sung. The ministers go in procession to the sanctuary if the sprinkling has been done from elsewhere in the church. The Collect follows, and the Ministry of the Word as usual.*

Tropes for the *Kyrie Eleison*

The acclamation Kyrie eleison *is common to nearly all Christian liturgies. It was most often used as a response for a litany. However, in the* Book of Common Prayer, *it was adapted to form a response to the Ten Commandments at the beginning of the Communion Service. In* Common Worship *it is used at the beginning of the Eucharist.*

The ancient Greek acclamation Kyrie eleison *was intended as an address to Christ, as the 'Kyrios' of Saint Paul's letters. In later (Western) usage it came to have a Trinitarian address, owing to the Latin adaptation* Christe eleison – *intended to make the christic address of the acclamation clear, but in fact having the longer-term effect of making the acclamation Trinitarian, with the first 'Kyrie' referring to the Father and the third to the Spirit. In the Middle Ages the Kyrie was 'troped' or interspersed with texts relating to the attributes of God, Christ, the Holy Spirit and the Blessed Virgin Mary.*

The Kyrie is a cry of acclamation, with the plea 'eleison' etymologically related to the Greek word for oil, suggesting that God is being asked to soothe and strengthen. It is hard to give the flavour of this in English translation, though it is usually translated as 'Lord have mercy'. This translation gives it a penitential flavour. However, even in English it is traditionally spoken as an exclamation rather than as a plea for pity: 'Lord have mercy upon us!'

The following tropes or verses to be sung with the Kyrie take up some of the scriptural titles and attributes of Christ. Some of the acclamations translated below are found in the Ambrosian Missal.

Between Epiphany and the Presentation of the Lord

Christ, made visible in the flesh: Lord, have mercy.
R/. Lord, have mercy
Lord, justified by the Spirit: Christ, have mercy.
R/. Christ, have mercy
Christ, proclaimed to the nations: Lord, have mercy.
R/. Lord, have mercy

Christ, believed in by the world:
Lord, professed by the Church:
Christ, taken up in glory:

Between the Presentation and Ash Wednesday and between Pentecost and All Saints' Day

Christ, image of the unseen God:
Lord, firstborn of all creation:
Christ, head of the body, the Church:

Christ, sent to heal the contrite:
Lord, who came to call sinners:
Christ, our advocate with the Father:

You came to gather the nations into the peace of God's kingdom:
You come in word and sacrament to strengthen us in holiness:
You will come in glory with salvation for your people:

You came to reconcile us to one another and to the Father:
You heal the wounds of sin and division:
You intercede for us at the throne of grace:

Lord Jesus, you healed the sick:
Lord Jesus, you forgave sinners:
Lord Jesus, you give us yourself to heal us and bring us strength:

Christ, sent to be our Saviour:
Lord, coming in humility:
Christ, friend of the poor:

You have the words of eternal life:
You are gentle and humble of heart:
You became obedient even to death:

You came from heaven to save us:
You died on the cross to give us life:
You rose from death as our promise of glory:

You came not to condemn but to forgive:
You rejoice in each repentant sinner:
You embrace us with the love of God:

You came to seek what was lost:
You gave your life as a ransom for all:
You gather together the scattered children of God:

Christ, fullness of truth and grace:
Lord who became poor to make us rich:
Christ, come to make us a holy people:

Between All Saints' Day and Advent

Christ, glorious in your saints:
Lord, strength of all who profess your name:
Christ, desire and goal of your disciples:

You are the eternal priest of the new covenant:
You build us into a holy temple for God:
You make us fellow citizens with the saints:

Christ, eternal Word:
Lord, teacher of truth:
Christ, giver of eternal life:

Son of God, who came to destroy sin and death:
Word of God, who delivered us from the fear of death:
Crucified Lord, forsaken in death, raised in glory:

Risen Lord, pattern of our life for ever:
Promise and image of what we shall be:
Origin and fulfilment of all things:

Kyrie Eleison as a Response to the Beatitudes

The use of the Kyrie as a response to the Commandments in the Prayer Book suggests that its use might be appropriate with other texts. Here is an adaptation for use with the Beatitudes (Matthew 5:3–12), which, as a liturgical canticle, are recommended in Common Worship *(p. 164) and also found in the Liturgy of the Orthodox Church.*

Blessed are the poor in spirit,
for theirs is the kingdom of heaven.
R/. Lord, have mercy, grant us this blessing.

Blessed are those who mourn,
for they shall be comforted.
R/. Lord, have mercy, grant us this blessing.

Blessed are the gentle,
for they shall inherit the earth.
R/. Lord, have mercy, grant us this blessing.

Blessed are those who hunger and thirst for justice,
for they shall be satisfied.
R/. Lord, have mercy, grant us this blessing.

Blessed are the merciful,
for they shall receive mercy.
R/. Lord, have mercy, grant us this blessing.

Blessed are the pure in heart,
for they shall see God.
R/. Lord, have mercy, grant us this blessing.

Blessed are the peacemakers,
for they shall be called the children of God.
R/. Lord, have mercy, grant us this blessing.

Blessed are those who are persecuted for the sake of justice,
for theirs is the kingdom of heaven.
R/. Lord, have mercy, grant us this blessing, Amen, Amen.

Kyrie Eleison as Part of a Litany

The following invocation might be used perhaps in procession, at the beginning of the service:

In the peace of Christ, let us pray to the Lord:
R/. Kyrie eleison.

For the peace that is from above and for the salvation of our lives,
let us pray to the Lord:
R/. Kyrie eleison.

For the peace of the whole world, the life of the churches and their unity,
let us pray to the Lord:
R/. Kyrie eleison.

That God will open our ears and hearts to receive the word of life,
let us pray to the Lord:
R/. Kyrie eleison.

That the Spirit will give us the words to praise the One who saves us:
let us pray to the Lord:
R/. Kyrie eleison.

(That Christ will welcome us to communion in his body and blood,
let us pray to the Lord:
R/. Kyrie eleison.)

That all who minister among us may serve the word of God,
let us pray to the Lord:
R/. Kyrie eleison.

That this day may be a day of rest and new life for all God's children,
let us pray to the Lord:
R/. Kyrie eleison.

That we who gather here may enter with joy into God's eternal kingdom,
let us pray to the Lord.
R/. Kyrie eleison.

All Saints' Day

As a significant date in the Calendar, marking the change from the summer 'Ordinary Time' to the Sundays before Advent, All Saints' Day may be marked with a processional entry for the Eucharist or Main Service.

The following Litany of Praise may be used. The responses are printed in italics:

Blessed be God, Father, Son and Holy Spirit:
And blessed be the Kingdom, now and for ever.

To the One who sits on the throne and to the Lamb:
Be glory and blessing, now and for ever.

To the One who is glorified in all the saints:
Be glory and blessing, now and for ever.

To the One who has called us to be holy:
Be glory and blessing, now and for ever.

The response is repeated after each of these commemorations.
If a shorter response is required, Thanks be to God *is suggested.*

For all those who have gone before us,
for Abraham and Sarah, our ancestors in faith,
journeying into the unknown yet trusting God's promises:

For Isaac and Jacob, the Patriarchs of Israel,
called to glorify God:

For Moses the Lawgiver and Aaron the Priest,
leaders of the people from slavery to freedom:

For Joshua, Gideon and the Judges,
obedient to God and trusting in his providence:

For Esther and Deborah, saviours of their nation,
who acted with courage for the name of God:

For Isaiah, Jeremiah and all the prophets,
who spoke of God's judgement and mercy:

For John the Baptist, the forerunner of Christ,
who rejoiced to see the Messiah come:

For Mary the Virgin, full of grace,
called to bear the Word Incarnate:

For Andrew and John and the first disciples,
who left all to follow Jesus:

For Peter and Paul, twin pillars of the Church,
who preached the gospel to Jew and gentile:

For Mary Magdalene, Salome and Mary,
the first witnesses and heralds of the resurrection:

For Matthew, Mark, Luke and John,
evangelists of the good news of Jesus Christ:

For Stephen the Deacon and James the Lord's Brother,
first among those who shed their blood for Christ:

For Alban, Julius and Aaron,
and all who witnessed to Christ even unto death:

For Augustine and Aidan, Boniface and Patrick,
and all who carried the gospel to this and other lands:

For Benedict and Francis, Hilda and Bede,
and for all who deepen our common life in Christ:

For Aelred and Bernard,
and all who live and teach the love of God:

For Anselm and Richard Hooker,
and for all who reveal the depths of God's wisdom:

For Julian of Norwich and Teresa of Avila,
and all who renew our vision of the mystery of God:

For Martin Luther, John Calvin and Thomas Cranmer,
and all who reform the Church of God:

For John Fisher and Thomas More,
and all who hold firm to its continuing faith:

For Gregory and Dunstan, George Herbert and John Keble,
and all who praise God in poetry and song:

For Lancelot Andrewes, John Wesley and Charles Simeon,
and for all who preach the word of God:

For William Wilberforce and Josephine Butler,
and all who work to bring justice to the world:

For Richard Challoner and John Henry Newman,
and all who nurture the faith of their fellow believers:

For Monica and for Mary Sumner,
and all who encourage faith in home or family:

For Oscar Romero and Janani Lwum,
and all the martyrs of our own time:

For all the unsung heroes of Christian faith,
whose names are known only to God:

For those who have been to us
as fathers and mothers in the faith of Christ:

The procession may end with the canticle Glory to God in the highest *and the Collect for All Saints' Day. The Ministry of the Word may then follow.*

Enthronement of the Gospels or Scriptures

From the time of the first ecumenical councils, it has been customary to bring the Book of Gospels into the worship space in procession and display or 'enthrone' it. The bishops of the Roman Catholic Church, gathered for the Second Vatican Council in 1963, enthroned the Gospels at the beginning of their deliberations, so as to put themselves in obedience to the word of Christ.

On Sundays, particularly if the Main Service is not the Eucharist, the ceremony of 'enthroning the scriptures', that is, bringing the Bible, Lectionary or Book of the Gospels into the congregation, might be appropriate.

The Entrance with the Holy Scriptures

Depending on which books are used, readers or other ministers may take part in the entrance procession carrying the books. The bearers may be accompanied by members of the congregation carrying lighted candles.

It might be appropriate to have a separate procession for the Scriptures, which might take a long route through the congregation to allow as many people as possible to come close to the Scriptures.

If a separate Book of the Gospels is used, it should come last in processional order.

Here are some of the many hymns that might be used:

Praise to you, O Christ our Saviour (Laudate 200)
God has spoken (Hymns for Today's Church 248)
Powerful in making us wise to salvation (Hymns for Today's Church 252)
Sow the Word (Gather 516)
Praise to God whose word was spoken (New English Hymnal 438)

The book(s) are placed in suitable locations in the worship area, perhaps upon lecterns or stands. Candles might be placed beside them.

The following responses might be used to end the rite:

V/. Blessed are you, God of all creation:
R/. Word by whom the universe was formed.

V/. Blessed are you, God of our salvation:
R/. Word made flesh in Jesus, child of Mary.

V/. Blessed are you, God of holiness:
R/. Holy Spirit, who speaks in the Scriptures.

or:

V/. In the beginning was the word:
R/. And the word was with God, and the word was God.
V/. By him all things came to be:
R/. In him was life, the light of mortals.
V/. The word was made flesh:
R/. And pitched a tent among us.
V/. We beheld his glory:
R/. The Father's only Son,
full of grace and truth.

One of the collects for Bible Sunday, pp. 152–3, may be used here.

For the *Agnus Dei*

The Agnus Dei *is also a litany, with* Have mercy on us *as its response.* Common Worship *gives two forms, with either of which the texts given here are compatible.*

Lamb of God *was introduced into the Roman Mass from the East, probably in the eighth century* CE. *It was a chant sung to cover the breaking of the eucharistic bread and pouring of the cups, a procedure that would originally have taken some time, as small leavened loaves were used and the wine had to be poured from one chalice into several smaller ones and mixed with wine that had not been 'consecrated'. To allow for this, the chant was simply extended, with as many repetitions of* Lamb of God . . . *as required.*

The Ambrosian Eucharist did not use the Agnus Dei. *To cover the breaking and preparation of the Communion, a chant known as* Confractorium *(i.e. 'for the breaking') was sung, which varied with the season or feast. As an alternative, some suggestions are made here for* Confractoria *– responsorial texts that refer directly to the action.*

Modern practice with the Agnus Dei, *where an extended setting is required, has been to 'trope' the text and vary the invocations. Some examples are given below. If they are to be sung, a simple setting of the petition* Have mercy on us *may be sung, and the invocation spoken or sung to a simple chant formula.*

V/. Lamb of God, you are our Passover and our peace:
R/. Have mercy on us.
V/. Lamb of God, you are our Sacrifice of reconciliation:
R/. Have mercy on us.
V/. Lamb of God, you are our great High Priest:
R/. Have mercy on us.

Lamb of God, true and living bread:
Lamb of God, true and lifegiving vine:
Lamb of God, food for our earthly pilgrimage:

Lamb of God, Shepherd of the flock:
Lamb of God, Shepherd who lays down his life:
Lamb of God, Risen Shepherd of souls:

Lamb of God, image and likeness of the Father:
Lamb of God, humbling yourself and accepting death:
Lamb of God, name above all names:

Anthems for the Breaking of the Bread

Christ our Passover is sacrificed for us:
Therefore let us keep the feast.
He is our peace, who has reconciled us to God:
Therefore let us keep the feast.
The marriage of the Lamb has come:
Therefore let us keep the feast.

The bread which we break
is a sharing in the body of Christ:
We being many are one body,
for we all share in the one bread.
Into one body we were all baptized,
and one Spirit was given us all to drink:
We being many are one body,
for we all share in the one bread.

My flesh is food indeed,
and my blood is drink indeed, says the Lord.
My flesh is food indeed,
and my blood is drink indeed, says the Lord.
Those who eat my flesh and drink my blood
dwell in me and I in them.
My flesh is food indeed,
and my blood is drink indeed, says the Lord.

Whoever eats this bread will live for ever:
Whoever eats this bread will live for ever.
The true bread comes down from heaven:
Whoever eats this bread will live for ever.
Whoever believes in me shall not hunger:
Whoever eats this bread will live for ever.

The disciples knew the Lord Jesus,
in the breaking of the bread.
The disciples knew the Lord Jesus,
in the breaking of the bread.
The bread which we break
is the communion of the body of Christ.
The disciples knew the Lord Jesus,
in the breaking of the bread.
We, though many, are one body,
for we all share in the one bread.
The disciples knew the Lord Jesus,
in the breaking of the bread.

Wisdom has prepared her table,
she has mixed her wine.
Blessed are those who are called
to the supper of the Lamb.
Come, eat of my bread,
and drink the wine I have prepared.
Blessed are those who are called
to the supper of the Lamb.
Listen to me and eat what is good,
delight yourselves in my rich food.
Blessed are those who are called
to the supper of the Lamb.

You shall eat and drink at my table in my kingdom,
says the Lord.
You shall eat and drink at my table in my kingdom,
says the Lord.
The Spirit and the Bride say 'Come.'
You shall eat and drink at my table in my kingdom,
says the Lord.
Let everyone who hears, say 'Come.'
You shall eat and drink at my table in my kingdom,
says the Lord.
Let everyone who is thirsty, come.
You shall eat and drink at my table in my kingdom,
says the Lord.

PART SIX

PROPER TEXTS FOR THE FESTIVALS DURING ORDINARY TIME

This section contains suggestions for the festivals and lesser festivals that fall between Epiphany and Lent and between Pentecost and Advent.

Each festival is assigned the following texts:

- some background information about the feast, which might be used to introduce the service
- a Scripture-related opening prayer
- a second collect as an alternative
- the verse for the Gospel Acclamation with *Alleluia*
- a collect to conclude the prayers of intercession
- a collect to conclude the preparing of the Lord's Table
- a proper thanksgiving or preface for the Eucharistic Prayer
- a collect for use after Communion

In the texts following, those days designated as 'festivals' have a full set of texts (Scripture-related opening prayer; opening prayer; Acclamation; Intercession; Prayer over the Gifts; Eucharistic Preface; Prayer after Communion) assigned to them. The 'lesser festivals' have a partial set (opening prayer; Acclamation; Intercession; Prayer over the Gifts; Eucharistic Preface; Prayer after Communion).

The texts for days designated as 'principal feasts' may be found among the Sunday propers.

Scripture-related opening prayers, like the Scripture readings, are on a single-year cycle.

25 January The Conversion of Saint Paul – Festival

This feast of Saint Paul seems to have originated in France in the fifth century. The liturgy celebrates God's free grace, the wonderful gift of God to the Apostolic Church in the person of Paul.

Scripture-related opening prayer

God of all wisdom,
who chose Saint Paul as an apostle
to proclaim the mystery of Christ
and to nurture your people in faith,
fill your Church with the same Spirit
that empowered his words,
and equip us for the ministry
of making known your salvation.
We ask this in the name of Jesus Christ,
who is one with you and the Holy Spirit,
God, blessed for ever and ever.

Opening prayer

God, strong and merciful,
you display the power of your compassion
in the conversion of sinners.
Let that same gracious gift
turn our hearts towards you,
just as it turned the Apostle Paul
from being a persecutor of your Church
into the chosen vessel for your word.
We make this prayer through Jesus Christ our Lord.

Acclamation

Jeremiah 1:5
V/. Alleluia, Alleluia, Alleluia.
R/. Alleluia, Alleluia, Alleluia.

V/. Before you were born I consecrated you:
I appointed you a prophet to the nations.
R/. Alleluia, Alleluia, Alleluia.

Intercession

Lord God,
in the preaching and work of Saint Paul
you showed us what the Church might truly be.
Keep us faithful to this vision
and centre us at all times
on the mystery of Christ among us.
We ask this in his name,
our Saviour for ever and ever.

Prayer over the Gifts

Gracious God,
keep us faithful to what we have received from the Lord,
so that when we break the one bread
we may be made one in the body of Christ,
whose name is glorified for ever and ever.

Eucharistic Preface

It is truly right and just, our joy and our salvation,
always and everywhere to give you thanks,
Lord, holy Father, almighty and eternal God.

You displayed the wonders of your grace
in your blessed Apostle Paul,
and chose him from his mother's womb,
that he should reveal your Son
and announce the good news to the gentiles.
He who had once been a blasphemer and persecutor
now showed himself so faithful in his ministry
that Christ Jesus himself made him

an example of patient service,
to instruct in the way of eternal life
all those who heard him and believed his word.

With him therefore,
we proclaim your mercy
in union with all the powers of heaven
in this, their joyful hymn of praise: Holy . . .

Prayer after Communion

Lord our God,
Let the holy gift we have received
kindle in us the fire of that same love
which filled the heart of your holy apostle Paul
with zealous care for all the churches.
We ask this through Christ our Lord.

26 January – Saints Timothy and Titus, Companions of Saint Paul – Lesser Festival

Timothy and Titus were disciples of Saint Paul. Two letters attributed to Paul are addressed to them. Eusebius' history of the Church records that Timothy was placed in charge of the church at Ephesus, where by tradition he was martyred for opposing the worship of Dionysus. By tradition, Titus was leader of the church in Crete.

Opening prayer

Lord God,
who endowed Saint Timothy and Saint Titus
with the power of the apostles;
grant through their example
that we may live justly and devoutly in this world
and come at last to our true home in heaven.

We ask this through Jesus Christ,
who is one with you and the Holy Spirit,
God, blessed for ever and ever.

Acclamation

Luke 10:2b
V/. Ask the Lord of the harvest:
to send labourers into his harvest.

Intercession

Loving Father,
let your Church be strong
in the grace of Jesus Christ,
to proclaim your time of favour
and to praise your steadfast love.
We ask this through Christ our Lord.

Prayer over the Gifts

Gracious God,
keep us faithful to what we have received from the Lord,
so that as we are to break the one bread
we may be made one in the body of Christ,
whose name is glorified for ever and ever.

Eucharistic Preface

We lift our hearts to you,
God everlasting, living and faithful;
to you we offer thanks and praise
through Jesus Christ your Son.

Through the gospel of Christ you set before us
the depths of your wisdom and love.
You set apart Saint Timothy and Saint Titus

to be preachers and heralds of that gospel
and teachers of the gentiles.

And so, with angels and all saints,
we glorify your holy name: Holy . . .

Prayer after Communion

Lord our God,
let the holy gift which we have received
nourish in us the same faith
which the apostles taught,
and which Saint Timothy and Saint Titus
maintained with such great care.
We ask this through Christ our Lord.

2 February The Presentation of the Lord in the Temple – Principal Feast

The texts for this day are found in the Sunday Propers, pp. 16–19.

1 March Saint David, Bishop, Patron of Wales – Lesser Festival

As David is a National Patron, a full set of texts is offered for this day.

Saint David, about whom little is known, belonged to the monastic movement linked with Gaul and Ireland, which was so influential in the coming of the Christian faith to Wales. Many churches across South Wales claim David as their founder. His chief foundation was at Mynyw (Menevia) in the far west of Dyfed. David was canonized by Pope Callistus II in 1123.

Scripture-related opening prayer

God, wellspring of holiness,
who gave to Saint David
the water of wisdom to drink,
open to us that same abundant fountain
that we may share his delight
in the lore and teaching of Christ.
We ask this in the name of Jesus
who is one with you and the Holy Spirit,
for ever and ever.

Opening prayer

O God,
who gave your servant David
the virtues of wisdom and eloquence,
making him an example of prayer and pastoral zeal;
grant that your Church, as the fruit of his teaching,
may grow in faith and give you joyful praise.
We ask this through Jesus Christ our Lord.

Acclamation

Psalm 67:3
V/. Let the peoples praise you, O God:
let all the peoples praise you.

Intercession

God our Father,
you gave the bishop David to the Welsh church
to uphold the faith
and to be an example of Christian perfection.
In this changing world, let his example help us
to hold fast the values that bring eternal life.
We ask this through Christ our Lord.

Prayer over the Gifts

Bring us, O God,
as joyful guests to your table,
and with the bread of your word
nourish in us
that faith which Saint David taught.
We ask this through Christ our Lord.

Eucharistic Preface

It is truly right and just, our duty and our salvation,
always and everywhere to give you thanks,
Lord, holy Father, almighty and eternal God,
through Jesus Christ our Lord.

Christ willed his Church to be the sign of salvation
when he sent forth apostles to announce the good news
and make all nations disciples of his teaching.
With eager heart, Saint David followed their example
and through his ministry planted your Church
among our ancestors in this land,
to open for them the way of salvation
through the life-giving mystery of Christ.

And so, with angels and all saints,
we exult and glorify your holy name: Holy . . .

Prayer after Communion

Almighty God,
grant that in the strength of this holy gift
we may follow Saint David
in seeking you above all things
and finding new life
in communion with Christ,
who is alive for ever and ever.

31 May The Visit of the Blessed Virgin Mary to Elizabeth – Festival

Saint Bonaventure introduced this feast into the Franciscan Calendar in the thirteenth century. In a typical Franciscan fashion, it celebrates the human emotions of Mary's visit to Elizabeth, as also the coming of the Holy Spirit of prophecy to reveal the presence of Christ and the grace given to the Virgin Mary.

Scripture-related opening prayer

God of wonders,
in the visitation of the blessed Virgin Mary
you brought joy to her kinswoman Elizabeth
as she greeted the mother of her Lord.
Let your Holy Spirit inspire in us
the same gladness as filled their meeting,
so that we may proclaim your greatness
as the God who exalts the lowly
and sets the needy in the place of princes.
This we ask through Jesus Christ,
who is one with you and the Holy Spirit
for ever and ever.

Opening prayer

Almighty and eternal God,
you inspired the Blessed Virgin Mary
while carrying your Son in her womb
to visit her cousin Elizabeth.
Grant that we also may be open
to follow the promptings of the Holy Spirit,
and with Mary, to glorify your holy name.
We ask this through Jesus Christ our Lord.

Acclamation

Luke 1:49
V/. The Mighty One has done great things for me:
and holy is his name.

Intercession

Be present in our midst, O God,
as you have promised to be with those who believe;
let your Church's prayer be heard
and your people's hands grow strong
to answer the needs of those
for whom we have offered our intercession.
We ask this through Christ our Lord.

Prayer over the Gifts

God of community,
as you brought Elizabeth and Mary together
in the praises of your mighty works,
so unite us now as we make thanksgiving
and give us the words to sing your praise.
We ask this through Christ our Lord.

Eucharistic Preface

It is truly right and just, our duty and our salvation,
always and everywhere to give you thanks,
Lord, holy Father, almighty and eternal God,
through Jesus Christ our Lord.

Through the prophetic words of Elizabeth
inspired by the Holy Spirit,
you revealed to us the greatness
bestowed on the Blessed Virgin Mary.
Rightly is she greeted as the blessed one
because she had believed the promise of salvation,

and, rightly welcomed for her kindly visit,
Mary is acclaimed as the mother of the Lord
by her who is to be the mother of his herald.

Therefore, with angels and saints,
we glorify your holy name: Holy . . .

Prayer after Communion

God of wonders,
Let your Church proclaim your greatness,
and the wonderful deeds you have done.
As John the Baptist leapt for joy
when he sensed the hidden presence of your Son,
so let your Church receive with gladness
the living presence of Christ in this sacrament.
We ask this through Christ our Lord.

Day of Thanksgiving for the Institution of Holy Communion – Optional Festival
Thursday after Trinity Sunday (Corpus Christi)

The feast of the Body and Blood of Christ originated in the thirteenth century, with a renewal of faith in the real presence of Christ in the Eucharist. It celebrates Christ's power to feed and nourish his people in their work of evangelism and reconciliation for the kingdom.

Opening prayer

Christ, our host,
who gave yourself to your disciples
as the food and drink of eternal life,
fill our hearts also with the bread of heaven
and slake our thirst with your spiritual cup,
so that our communion with you

may bear fruit in works of love and service.
For you are the life of your people, for ever and ever.

Acclamation

John 6:57
V/. 'Just as the living Father sent me, and I live because of the Father:
so whoever eats me will live because of me,' says the Lord.

Intercession

God of infinite goodness,
from the very beginning of your Church
you have renewed the faith of your people
through communion with the body and blood of Christ.
May the sacrament of your love
sustain us as we journey towards the day
when this mystery will stand unveiled
for ever and ever.

Prayer over the Gifts

Gracious God,
bestow upon your Church
the gifts of unity and peace,
now pledged for us in this bread and cup.
We ask this through Christ our Lord.

Eucharistic Preface

We lift our hearts to you,
God most blessed, faithful and eternal;
to you we offer thanks and praise
through Jesus Christ your Son.

As he ate with his disciples at the Last Supper,
Jesus gave himself up to you

as the Lamb without blemish,
the sacrifice that renders you perfect praise.
He chose to continue through all time
the memorial of his passion and cross.
In this holy sacrament
you feed your people and make them holy,
so that the human race that shares this one earth
may share also the light of one faith
and be joined in one great bond of love.

Earth unites with heaven
in this new and eternal shout of praise: Holy . . .

Prayer after Communion

Bring us, O Christ,
to that eternal union with you
which is foreshadowed here on earth
by our communion in your body and blood,
for you are alive,
our Saviour, for ever and ever.

11 June Saint Barnabas the Apostle – Festival

Barnabas, a Jew of Cypriot birth, was a leading member of the church at Jerusalem, though not himself one of the Twelve. The Book of Acts records that he introduced Saint Paul to the community and afterwards worked with Paul in Antioch and on his missionary journey. Tradition recounts how his relics were discovered on this day, some time in the fifth century.

Scripture-related opening prayer

God, source of all courage,
who through the Apostle Barnabas
gave new heart to your Church;

let those you call to be Christians
have boldness to speak your word
and ready hands to help the needy,
for the praise of Jesus, your Son,
who is one with you and the Holy Spirit
for ever and ever.

Opening prayer

O God, you commanded that Saint Barnabas,
a man filled with faith and the Holy Spirit,
should be set apart for the conversion of the nations.
Grant that the gospel of Christ
which he preached with boldness
may be faithfully proclaimed in word and deed.
We ask this through Jesus Christ our Lord.

Acclamation

John 15:15
V/. 'I have called you friends,' says the Lord:
'because I have made known to you
everything I have learned from my Father.'

Intercession

God, who made Saint Barnabas
the companion of the apostles in preaching the gospel,
grant, we pray, that as we celebrate his festival,
so we may come to share his inheritance in your glory.
Through Christ our Lord.

Prayer over the Gifts

Bless, Lord, the table we have prepared
and through our communion with you
kindle in us that same love

which inspired Saint Barnabas
to bring the light of the gospel to the nations.
This we ask through Christ our Lord.

Eucharistic Preface

It is truly right and just, our duty and our salvation,
always and everywhere to give you thanks,
Lord, holy Father, almighty and eternal God.

By the voice of your Holy Spirit you chose Saint Barnabas
from the assembly of those who believed in Christ.
You numbered him among the apostles
as the companion of Saint Paul,
sending him to minister the truth of your gospel
so that salvation and eternal life
might be announced to all the nations.

And so, with angels and all saints
we sing the unceasing hymn of your glory: Holy . . .

Prayer after Communion

Lord God,
we have received the gifts that pledge eternal life
on this feast of the Apostle Barnabas.
Grant that we may one day behold in its fullness
the mystery which we celebrate in sacrament and sign.
We ask this through Jesus Christ our Lord.

24 June The Birth of Saint John the Baptist – Festival

It is known that a feast of Saint John the Baptist was celebrated on this date as early as the fourth century. It celebrates John as the 'forerunner' of Christ, the herald who announced his presence and baptized him in the Jordan.

Scripture-related opening prayer

God of justice,
who in the appearing of John the Baptist
prepared the way for the advent of your Christ,
grant that just as his birth empowered the dumb to speak,
so also your grace may inspire your people
and open their hearts to your strong and gentle mercy.
We ask this in the name of Jesus Christ,
who is one with you and the Holy Spirit,
for ever and ever.

Opening prayer

God of all consolation,
grant that as we celebrate the birth of John the Baptist,
the preacher of repentance and herald of the Saviour,
so we may be challenged by his call to conversion
and comforted by the salvation
whose advent he proclaimed.
We ask this through Jesus Christ our Lord.

Acclamation

Luke 1:76
V/. You, child, will be called the Prophet of the Most High:
for you will go before the Lord to prepare his ways.

Intercession

God, our desire,
keep your Church alert and waiting for you,
ready to recognize you whenever you come:
in mercy and forgiveness,
in the nearness of the poor,
the darkness of prison
and the witness of the martyr.
Let our prayer always be

that your rule may be established,
for ever and ever.

Prayer over the Gifts

God, be present
as we come to this holy table,
and by the sacrament we celebrate
make us a people prepared for the Lord,
who is alive, now and for ever.

Eucharistic Preface

We lift our hearts to you,
God eternal, living and true;
to you we offer thanks and praise
through Jesus Christ our Lord.

At the birth of John the Baptist
his father's tongue was loosed
to sing with joy of your praise and glory.
Greatest and last of the prophets,
John became the herald of Christ your Son
who counted him the greatest
of all those born of woman.

In that same joy which graced his birth,
we now rejoice with angels and saints
in this, their ageless hymn of praise: Holy . . .

Prayer after Communion

Eternal God,
you have blessed us
with the heavenly feast of the Lamb.
Let our joy be that of John, his herald,
and our work be to proclaim the kingdom
where Christ is Lord, for ever and ever.

29 June Saint Peter and Paul, Apostles – Festival

By tradition, Saint Peter and Saint Paul were martyred in Rome at the same time, between 64 and 67 CE. Their joint feast was first celebrated in Rome, as the patronal feast of the Roman church, from as early as the third century. The two apostles are often depicted together, differing in appearance, temperament and mission, but united by their faith, in their death and their veneration.

Scripture-related opening prayer

God of salvation,
in the witness of Peter and the preaching of Paul
you have poured out an oil of gladness
to kindle the flame of faith among your people.
Let that fire burn strongly in your Church,
that we may proclaim the message of salvation
and attain to the blessings of your kingdom.
This we ask through Jesus Christ,
who is one with you and the Holy Spirit,
for ever and ever.

Opening prayer

Lord our God,
you give us this joyful day of celebration
to honour the Apostles Peter and Paul.
Grant that as your Church received from them
the first foundations of its faith,
so it may in all things remain true to their teaching.
This we ask through Jesus Christ our Lord.

Acclamation

Zechariah 4:14
V/. Behold, the two anointed ones:
who stand by the Lord of the whole earth.

Intercession

Lord Jesus,
Peter denied you and Paul persecuted you,
yet you made them witnesses
of your love and your truth.
Continually transform us as you look on us,
that your power may be at its fullest in our weakness;
then in union with the apostles
we shall glorify our God and Father,
for ever and ever.

Prayer over the Gifts

We prepare your holy table, Lord,
in fellowship with the Apostles Peter and Paul,
knowing that of ourselves we can do nothing,
but ready to praise you who have brought us salvation.
Through Christ our Lord.

Eucharistic Preface

It is truly right and just, our duty and our salvation,
always and everywhere to give you thanks,
Lord, holy Father, almighty and eternal God.

Your holy apostles, Peter and Paul,
fill us with praise for your plan of salvation.
Peter it was who first professed the faith
and Paul who unfolded it for our understanding.
Peter brought together the earliest Church
from the remnant of Israel's flock,
while Paul became your interpreter,
the teacher of gentiles whom you had called.
In differing ways they gathered one people for Christ;
one martyrs' crown they shared
and are honoured as one throughout the world.

And therefore, with angels and all saints,
we exult and glorify your holy name: Holy . . .

Prayer after Communion

Lord, renew the life of your Church
by the celebration of this sacrament;
keep us faithful to the breaking of bread
and the teaching of the apostles,
that we may be one in heart and soul,
sealed and confirmed by your love.
We ask this through Christ our Lord.

When Saint Peter only is to be commemorated

By divine inspiration, Peter, the fisherman of Galilee, confessed Jesus as the Christ, the Son of God. Jesus spoke of him as 'the rock' on which the Church was to be built. On Pentecost Day he was the first to address the people and proclaim the risen Christ (Acts 2:14–36). Two letters in the New Testament bear his name.

Scripture-related opening prayer

Living God,
who entrusted to Peter
the power of binding and loosing;
keep your Church faithful to this mission,
that oppressors may be confronted
and those who carry heavy burdens be set free.
We ask this in the name of Christ, the Saviour,
who is one with you and the Holy Spirit,
for ever and ever.

Opening prayer

God of truth,
you have built your Church
upon the rock of that same faith
which Peter professed in Christ, your Son.
Grant that nothing may disturb or shake
this blessing which you have revealed to us.
This we ask through Jesus Christ, our Lord.

Acclamation

Matthew 16:16
V/. Peter said: 'You are the Christ:
the Son of the living God.'

Intercession

God, searcher of hearts,
who called Peter the fisherman
to gather together a great multitude of believers;
let your Church never fail
to welcome such a diversity of people
and to rejoice in the many gifts of those
whom you have brought together
to acknowledge and praise your holy name.
We ask this through Christ our Lord.

Prayer over the Gifts

God, our strength,
you kept Saint Peter faithful
in his witness to you through suffering.
As we celebrate his memory
open our lips in your praise
and lift our hearts to you in Peter's faith.
We ask this through Christ our Lord.

Eucharistic Preface

It is truly right and just, our duty and our salvation,
always and everywhere to give you thanks,
Lord, holy Father, almighty and eternal God.

You chose Peter to be the first of the disciples
to profess faith in Jesus as your Son and Messiah,
and on that same faith Christ promised
that he would build his Church.
Your Son entrusted to Peter the keys of the kingdom
and, though Peter had denied him, prayed for him,
that he might have the power
to strengthen the faith of his brothers and sisters.

And so, for the honour you gave to Saint Peter
we celebrate his feast with all the hosts of angels
in this, their joyful hymn of praise: Holy . . .

Prayer after Communion

Lord God,
you have made us guests at the banquet of salvation
to honour the memory of the Apostle Peter.
In thanksgiving we ask you:
keep us close to your Son,
who alone has the words of life,
that he may lead us as faithful sheep of your flock
to the eternal pastures of heaven,
where he lives and reigns for ever and ever.

3 July Saint Thomas the Apostle – Festival

Thomas, 'The Twin', was one of the Twelve chosen by Christ. He is remembered for the incident of his doubting the resurrection and then expressing faith in the words 'My Lord and my God'(John 20:28). Tradition makes him the Apostle of India, where sites connected with him are still places of pilgrimage.

Scripture-related opening prayer

God of all truth,
who brought your Apostle Thomas
from doubt into faith
as he set eyes on the body of the risen Christ;
grant that we, who have not seen,
may share the wonder and joy
of his faith in Christ as Lord and God.
We ask this in the name of Jesus,
the name that brings salvation
for ever and ever.

Opening prayer

Almighty God,
as we honour the feast of Saint Thomas the Apostle,
let his example strengthen our faith,
that we also may acknowledge
Jesus Christ as our Lord and God,
and, believing, may have life in his name:
who lives and reigns with you and the Holy Spirit,
for ever and ever.

Acclamation

cf. Ephesians 2:20
V/. You are built upon the foundation of the apostles and prophets:
with Christ Jesus himself as the cornerstone.

Intercession

God of salvation,
let the faith of Saint Thomas
give strength to your Church,
that as he acknowledged your Son as Lord and God,
so we also may find life in his name,
who lives and reigns for ever and ever.

Prayer over the Gifts

Lord God,
on the feast of Saint Thomas
we celebrate the sacrifice of praise.
Hear our prayers
and protect the gifts of grace
you have bestowed upon your people.
This we ask through Christ our Lord.

Eucharistic Preface

We lift our hearts to you,
God, ever true and faithful;
to you we offer thanks and praise
in the name of Jesus Christ your Son.

After his rising from the dead,
Christ appeared first to the disciples
in the absence of Thomas,
so that later, freed from unbelief,
Thomas might touch the risen One
and so strengthen the faith of those who believe.
He acknowledged the true body of his Master,
believed in him as God and acclaimed him as Lord
and so became a faithful witness to the resurrection.

Therefore, with angels and saints,
we exult and glorify your holy name: Holy . . .

Prayer after Communion

Grant, O God,
that as in this sacrament
we receive the body of Christ your Son,
so by our lives and conduct
we may acknowledge him as our God,
whom now, like Thomas,

we know by faith.
We ask this through Christ our Lord.

11 July Saint Benedict, Abbot – Lesser Festival

Saint Benedict was born in Norcia, Umbria, in about 480 and died at Monte Cassino about 547. As a young man he became a hermit at Subiaco, but later formed communities of disciples. For one of these he wrote his 'Rule' by which Benedictine communities, and many others, still live. Since 1964 he has been honoured as a Patron Saint of Europe.

A recommended selection of Scripture readings is:

OT: Proverbs 2:1–11
Psalm: 119 vv. 33–40
NT: Colossians 3:12–17
Gospel: Matthew 6:25–34

Opening prayers

The first opening prayer is based upon a prayer for Vespers which echoes themes from Saint Benedict's Rule.

Ever-faithful God,
through the teaching of Saint Benedict
you enable men and women to walk the way of life
under the guidance of the gospel.
In your mercy, bring to completion
the work you have begun in all of us,
and lead us to your holy dwelling place,
where you are glorified evermore
through Jesus Christ,
who is one with you and the Holy Spirit,
for ever and ever.

or:

Open our ears, most gentle God,
that we may hear and heed
your call to us to become your disciples.
With Saint Benedict as our example
grant that we may live together
in mutual charity and peace,
as befits those whom you have named
your beloved children in Christ,
who lives and reigns for ever and ever.

Acclamation

Matthew 6:33
V/. 'Strive first for the kingdom of God:
and for his righteousness,' says the Lord.

Intercession

Almighty and eternal God,
who showed us the path of humility
in the teaching of the holy Abbot Benedict,
grant, we pray,
that strengthened by his example
we may walk that way with ever-joyful hearts.
We ask this through Christ our Lord.

Prayer over the Gifts

Look upon us, Lord,
as we come to your altar
to give thanks on this feast of Saint Benedict.
Grant that by following his example in seeking you,
we may receive in your service
the gifts of unity and peace.
We ask this through Christ our Lord.

Eucharistic Preface

It is truly right and just, our duty and our salvation,
always and everywhere to give you thanks,
Lord, holy Father, almighty and eternal God.

You bestowed on Saint Benedict
rich gifts of the Holy Spirit,
making him the father
of a great company of the just,
and an outstanding teacher
of love for you and our neighbour.
In his holy Rule, with a clear and wise discretion,
he taught men and women to walk the way of salvation
under the guidance of Christ and the gospel,
and now he is revered as the patron
of a multitude of nations.

And so, with angels and saints,
we glorify your holy name: Holy . . .

Prayer over the Gifts

We pray to you, O God,
that we who have received the pledge of eternal life
may follow the counsels of Saint Benedict
in being faithful to the work of your praise
and serving one another in true charity.
We make this prayer through Jesus Christ our Lord.

22 July Saint Mary Magdalen – Festival

According to the Fourth Gospel, Mary Magdalen, a disciple of Christ, was the first to meet the Risen Christ and announced to the apostles that Christ was risen (John 20:17–18). In the Eastern churches, Mary Magdalen is known as the 'Apostle to the apostles'.

Scripture-related opening prayer

God, our beloved,
grant that as Mary Magdalen
heard her name spoken by the risen Christ,
so also we may listen for you
to speak our name and raise us up in faith;
then shall we give you thanks,
our help, our joy and our God,
through Jesus Christ,
who is one with you and the Holy Spirit,
for ever and ever.

Opening prayer

Lord God,
whose only-begotten Son
entrusted first to Mary Magdalen
the joyful news of Easter;
grant, through her example,
that we may proclaim the living Christ
and behold him in the glory of your kingdom,
where he lives and reigns for ever and ever.

Acclamation

John 20:18
V/. Mary Magdalen went and announced to the disciples:
'I have seen the Lord.'

Intercession

Lord,
let the example of Saint Mary Magdalen
be a strength and help to your Church,
for she, delivered from the power of demons,
placed herself at the disposal of Christ
who had set her free.
We ask this through Christ our Lord.

Prayer over the Gifts

Accept, Lord, our worship
on this feast of Saint Mary Magdalen,
just as your Son accepted
the service of love that she offered.
We ask this through Jesus Christ our Lord.

Eucharistic Preface

It is truly right and just, our duty and our salvation,
always and everywhere to give you thanks,
Lord, holy Father, almighty and eternal God,
through Jesus Christ our Lord.

You kindled in the heart of Mary Magdalen
a love for Christ whose word had set her free
from the evil spirit that had oppressed her.
You gave her the courage of love
to follow him even to the cross.
You made her the first
to behold him, risen from the dead,
and the first to announce to the apostles
that Christ was risen to new and glorious life.
Her words still ring throughout the Church,
to strengthen the faith and encourage the hope
of those who gather faithfully for prayer.

And so, with angels and saints,
we glorify your holy name:

Prayer after Communion

Lord God,
as we receive this sacrament,
fill us with that persevering love
which kept Saint Mary Magdalen
faithful to Christ, her risen Master,
who lives and reigns for ever and ever.

25 July Saint James, Apostle – Festival

James, the brother of John, is recorded as the first apostle to die for his faith in Christ (Acts 12:2). He was evidently a favoured disciple, as he was present at the Transfiguration (Matthew 17:1), the raising of Jairus' daughter (Luke 8:51) and the garden of Gethsemane (Matthew 26:36). He is to be distinguished from the James who was the brother of Philip and the James known as 'The Lord's Brother'.

Scripture-related opening prayer

God, our salvation,
who called the Apostle James
to witness the glory of your Son
and to drink the cup of his Master's suffering,
grant that we, as Christ's disciples
may not fear to profess the name of Jesus,
and may show his love in service of our neighbour,
so that in our flesh also
the life of Jesus may be manifest.
We ask this in his name
who is Lord for ever and ever.

Opening prayer

Almighty and eternal God,
you consecrated the labours of the apostles
by the martyrdom of Saint James,
the first among them to shed his blood for Christ.
Grant that his witness
and patient endurance of suffering
may give strength and vigour to your Church.
We ask this through Christ our Lord.

Acclamation

Matthew 20:28
V/. The Son of Man came not to be served but to serve:
and to give his life as a ransom for many.

Intercession

Grant, we pray you, Lord,
that as we now rejoice
in this commemoration of your Apostle Saint James,
so with him we may have eternal gladness
at the sight of your glory, face to face.
We ask this through Christ our Lord.

Prayer over the Gifts

Lord,
cleanse us in the saving baptism
which is the passion of Christ,
so that in fellowship with Saint James
we may drink without fear
the cup our Saviour holds out to us.
through Christ our Lord.

Eucharistic Preface

It is truly right and just, our duty and our salvation,
always and everywhere to give you thanks,
Lord, holy Father, almighty and eternal God,
through Jesus Christ our Lord.

Christ called Saint James from mending fishing nets
to make him a fisherman of salvation.
As James was ready and faithful in all things,
Christ made him the first among the apostles
to undergo the suffering
and receive the glory of a martyr's death.

And so, with angels and saints,
we glorify your holy name: Holy . . .

Prayer after Communion

As we have now received the cup of the Lord,
so prepare us, O God,
by the example of Saint James,
to witness to your mighty works
knowing that nothing can separate us
from your love revealed in Christ,
who is alive for ever and ever.

26 July Saint Anne and Saint Joachim, Parents of the Blessed Virgin Mary – Lesser Festival

According to a second-century tradition, Joachim and Anne were the parents of the Blessed Virgin Mary. Their feast came to the West from the Eastern churches. Saint Anne was first commemorated in the Latin churches in the eighth century, Joachim in the fifteenth century.

Opening prayer

Lord, God of our forebears,
you chose your servants Anne and Joachim
to be the parents of Mary,
Mother of your incarnate Son.
In them we acknowledge your faithfulness;
so let us also grow in trust
that you will fulfil all that you have promised.
We ask this through Jesus Christ,
who is one with you and the Holy Spirit,
for ever and ever.

Acclamation

Zechariah 2:10
V/. 'Sing and rejoice, O daughter Zion:
for I will come and dwell in your midst,' says the Lord.

Intercession

All-knowing God,
who chose us in Christ
to be your people,
make your Church worthy of its calling.
We ask this through Christ our Lord.

Prayer over the Gifts

God of blessing,
whose love has brought us to prepare your table,
grant that here we may share in those good things
promised to Abraham and to his descendants for ever,
through Christ our Lord.

Eucharistic Preface

It is truly right and just, our duty and our salvation,
always and everywhere to give you thanks,
Lord, holy Father, almighty and eternal God.

On this feast of Saint Anne and Saint Joachim
we glorify you, and in their memorial
we praise the loving purpose of your wisdom
which brought salvation to the human race.
Of old you promised a saviour,
and for the wondrous fulfilment of that promise
you granted to these parents
a holy child, the Virgin Mary,
by whom you have given us Christ your Son,
in the wonder of the Incarnation.

And so, with angels and saints,
we glorify your holy name: Holy . . .

Prayer after Communion

God of wonders,
you chose that your Son
should be born into a human family,
so that we might be reborn of you.
As you have nourished us at your table,
so make us holy by that same Spirit
through whom we are adopted as your sons and daughters.
We ask this through Christ our Lord.

29 July Mary, Martha and Lazarus, Companions of Our Lord – Lesser Festival

Mary and Martha, sisters, together with Lazarus their brother, lived at Bethany. They are remembered for their hospitality to Jesus. By tradition, Mary is remembered as the one who sat at his feet (Luke 10:39) and Martha for her confession of faith in him before he raised Lazarus from the dead (John 11:27).

Opening prayer

Almighty and eternal God,
whose Son honoured the home
of Mary, Martha and Lazarus
by coming there as a guest;
make us, we pray you, faithful servants of Christ
in love and care for our neighbour,
and welcome us one day
into your dwelling place in heaven.
Through Jesus, your Christ,
who is one with you and the Holy Spirit,
for ever and ever.

Acclamation

Isaiah 25:9
V/. Lo! This is our God, for whom we have waited:
so that he might save us.

Intercession

Let your Church praise you, O God,
in hope and trust,
and become, for all men and women,
a place of deliverance and new life.
We ask this through Christ our Lord.

Prayer over the Gifts

At this table, O God,
bestow upon us that communion in the Spirit
by which our service of you
may be inspired and nourished.
We ask this through Jesus Christ our Lord.

Eucharistic Preface

It is truly right and just
that heaven and earth should praise you, O God,
for your faithfulness and steadfast love.

We celebrate Christ the King of heaven,
who came to the home of Mary, Martha and Lazarus
with gifts of wisdom, faith and life out of death.

And so, with angels and all saints
we glorify your holy name: Holy . . .

Prayer after Communion

God of serenity,
let this sharing in the gifts of your love

dispose our hearts to listen to you,
our wills to trust in you
and our lives to be renewed
by your liberating Spirit.
We ask this through Christ our Lord.

6 August The Transfiguration of the Lord – Festival

This feast originated as the dedication festival of the Transfiguration Church on Mount Tabor. It appeared in the Latin-speaking Church in the eighth century and in the fifteenth century became part of the calendar of the whole Western Church.

6 August is also the anniversary of the dropping of the atomic bomb on Hiroshima in 1945. Many churches commemorate this event on this day.

Scripture-related opening prayer

Eternal God,
who revealed the glory of your Son
to his chosen witnesses on the holy mountain,
make us attentive to his presence among us,
that with them, we may gaze in silence and wonder
at him whose full glory we hope one day to see,
Jesus Christ, who is one with you and the Holy Spirit,
for ever and ever.

Opening prayer

God of light and truth,
in the transfiguration of your Son
you strengthened faith in him
by the witness of your prophets
and wonderfully foreshadowed

our adoption as your children;
grant that we, your people
may heed the voice of Jesus
and become heirs with him to eternal glory.
We ask this through Jesus Christ our Lord.

Acclamation

Luke 9:35
V/. From the cloud came a voice that said:
'This is my Son, my Chosen. Listen to him!'

Intercession

God our Father,
you shed light for the disciples
on Christ's way of the cross;
let our eyes reflect that light,
and our hearts retain the sound of his voice,
that we may turn to our neighbour
and share the love with which you fill us.
We ask this through Christ our Lord.

Additional intercession for Hiroshima Day

Christ, our only true light,
before whose bright cloud
your friends fell to the ground;
we bow before your cross
that we may remember in our bodies
the dead who fell like shadows;
and that we may refuse to be prostrated
before the false brightness
of any other light,
looking to your power alone
for hope of resurrection from the dead.

Prayer over the Gifts

Holy God,
make this table holy
which you have prepared for us,
and bring us to that glory
which we see in the face of Christ,
who is Lord for ever and ever.

Eucharistic Preface

It is truly right and just, our duty and our salvation,
always and everywhere to give you thanks,
Lord, holy Father, almighty and eternal God,
through Jesus Christ our Lord.

Christ revealed his glory before chosen witnesses
and filled with splendour
that human form in which he is one with us.
In this way he prepared the disciples
to bear the scandal of the cross
and showed that in the Church, his body,
the same glory would be fulfilled
that shone out from him, the head.

And so, with angels and all saints
we glorify your holy name: Holy . . .

Prayer after Communion

God, our glory,
who in the face of Christ
have revealed your true likeness,
transform us, who share this food from heaven,
so that as members of his body
we may be partakers of the divine nature.
This we ask through Christ our Lord.

15 August The Blessed Virgin Mary – Festival

A feast of the Virgin Mary was kept on this date as early as the fifth century in Jerusalem, commemorating her 'Falling Asleep'. Under the influence of an ancient legend, which told of the apostles assembling for her death and then finding her coffin empty, it became a feast of her 'Assumption into Heaven'. In the Church of England Calendar this festival functions as a generic commemoration of the Blessed Virgin Mary, without any particular legendary or doctrinal references being implied.

Scripture-related opening prayer

God, whose mercy is from age to age,
we praise you for the working of your grace
in Mary, Mother of the Incarnate Word.
As she has been welcomed into your heavenly dwelling,
so let our hearts be set heavenward,
and our lives be open to the power of your Spirit,
so that with Mary we may glorify your name for ever.
We ask this through Jesus Christ our Lord,
who is one with you and the Holy Spirit,
for ever and ever.

Opening prayer

God, our greatest joy,
by whose choice
Mary, the lowly woman of Nazareth,
embraced your eternal Word
as the son of her womb,
let us rejoice to call her blessed
and glorify you
who have worked in her such wonders.
We ask this through Christ our Lord.

Intercession

In her humility and obedience to your calling, O God,
the Virgin Mary stands as a model for your Church.
Grant that your people may trust in your word,
and so in faith become bearers of Christ,
our light and our life, for ever and ever.

Prayer over the Gifts

We offer you, Lord,
the sacrifice of praise
as we honour the Mother of your Son;
grant that through this holy exchange
we may be made an everlasting gift to you.
We ask this through Christ our Lord.

Eucharistic Preface

It is truly right and just, our duty and our salvation,
to proclaim the marvels which you our God
have worked among your people,
and with the Blessed Virgin Mary
to sing the praises of your holy name,
and glorify your steadfast love.

Truly, you work wonders over all the earth,
and from age to age extend your gracious mercy.
You looked with favour on your lowly servant
and through her you gave to the world
Jesus Christ your Son,
the author of life and salvation.

And so, with angels and all saints,
we proclaim your glory
in their unceasing hymn of praise: Holy . . .

Prayer after Communion

O God,
you have made us partakers
in the food of heaven.
On this feast of blessed Mary,
let us rejoice in the fullness of your grace
and your desire to fill us with your gift of salvation.
We ask this through Christ our Lord.

24 August Saint Bartholomew, Apostle – Festival

Bartholomew is often identified with Nathaniel of Cana, whom Jesus described as the 'Israelite without guile' (John 1:47). He is associated by tradition with the beginnings of Christianity in India and Armenia, where he is said to have met a martyr's death.

Scripture-related opening prayer

Loving God,
who called the apostles
to be companions of Christ
and witnesses to his resurrection;
grant that as we remember Saint Bartholomew
we may heed the calling
to humility and service
which is Christ's will for his whole Church.
We ask this in his name,
for he is one with you and the Holy Spirit,
for ever and ever.

Opening prayer

God, our Saviour,
strengthen in us that faith
which bound the Apostle Bartholomew to your Son,

so that your Church may become for all peoples
the sacrament of your salvation.
We ask this through Jesus Christ our Lord.

Acclamation

Luke 22:28, 29
V/. 'You are those,' said the Lord:
who have stood by me in my trials.'

Intercession

God, who built your Church
on the foundation of the apostles,
enrich your people by their example
and nourish our faith through their teaching,
that we may bear witness to Christ,
and find in you our true home for ever.
We ask this through Christ our Lord.

Prayer over the Gifts

God of praise,
send the Holy Spirit,
which you poured out upon the apostles,
that we may acclaim the word of truth
which we have received through them,
and joyfully return thanks to your glory.
We ask this through Christ our Lord.

Eucharistic Preface

It is truly right and just, our duty and our salvation,
always and everywhere to give you thanks,
Lord, holy Father, almighty and eternal God.

We praise and bless you on this day
as we honour your Apostle Bartholomew,

who followed the footsteps of Christ his Master
and for his sake did not hesitate to shed his blood.
Now, his torments over, he holds the victor's palm
and invites us to share his own all-conquering faith.

And so, with angels and all saints,
we glorify your holy name: Holy . . .

Prayer after Communion

Grant, O God,
that we who remember your Apostle Bartholomew
may be sustained and nourished now and always
by this pledge of eternal salvation which we have received.
We ask this through Christ our Lord.

29 August The Beheading of Saint John the Baptist – Lesser Festival

The Gospels record the execution of John (Matthew 14, Mark 6). The Jewish classical historian Josephus locates the event at the fortress of Machaerus near the Dead Sea. The origin of this feast may lie in the dedication festival of a church dedicated to John the Baptist at Sebaste, in Palestine, where he is reputedly buried.

Opening prayer

God of prophets,
let the example of John the Baptist
keep us true to your name,
so that in us Christ may increase and we decrease,
and you may be our joy and crown.
We ask this through Jesus Christ,
who is one with you and the Holy Spirit,
God, for ever and ever.

Acclamation

Psalm 11:9
V/. The Lord is righteous, he loves righteous deeds:
and those who are upright shall behold his face.

Intercession

You surround us, O God,
with a great cloud of witnesses.
Let your Church on earth
be lifted up in hope and praise
to set its heart with your Church in heaven.
We ask this through Christ our Lord.

Prayer over the Gifts

Lord,
through the Eucharist
keep us faithful to the path of righteousness
which John the Baptist taught
and to which he bore witness
by shedding his blood.
We ask this through Jesus Christ our Lord.

Eucharistic Preface

It is truly right and just, our duty and our salvation,
always and everywhere to give you thanks,
Lord, holy Father, almighty and eternal God,
through Jesus Christ our Lord.

You chose John the Baptist
to be the herald and forerunner of Christ;
you gave him the honour
of baptizing Jesus in the Jordan,
and announcing him as the Lamb
who by dying would take away our sins.

You found John worthy
of accepting baptism in his own blood,
by dying a martyr's death
to complete his witness to your Son.

And so, with angels and saints,
we glorify your holy name: Holy . . .

Prayer after Communion

Faithful God,
as we honour the birth into eternal life
of Saint John the Baptist,
grant that in the conduct of our lives
we may honour the sacrament we have received
and experience the workings of its grace.
This we ask through Christ our Lord.

8 September Nativity of the Blessed Virgin Mary – Lesser Festival

This feast originated in Jerusalem in the sixth century, and within a century appeared in the Roman Calendar.

The scriptural inspiration for the Scripture-related opening prayer is taken from those readings suggested for both the Nativity and the Conception of the Blessed Virgin Mary. As this feast is often used in the Church of England as the generic commemoration of Mary in preference to 15 August, a full set of texts is suggested here.

Scripture-related opening prayer

Faithful God,
who promised to Adam that his seed
should crush the serpent's head,

grant that as we have seen your promise fulfilled
in the coming of Christ, your Son and child of Adam,
so also we may find joy
in the birth of Mary, who was to bear him
and present him to the world.
We ask this in his name,
who is one with you and the Holy Spirit,
for ever and ever.

Opening prayer

Grant to your people, Lord, this gift of grace:
that as our salvation was begun
in the birth of your Son from the Virgin Mary,
so this celebration of her nativity
may make us grow in your peace.
We ask this through Jesus Christ our Lord.

Acclamation

Luke 1:49
V/. The Mighty One has done great things for me:
and holy is his name.

Intercession

Lord God, you created Mary
to share in the wonderful mystery
of the union in Jesus
of your divinity and her humanity.
Grant that, following her example,
we too may let your power
dwell in our poverty.
Hear our prayer, you who are God,
blessed for ever and ever.

Prayer over the Gifts

As we celebrate with joy
the birth of the Blessed Virgin Mary,
we humbly pray you, Lord God,
that as your Son took his human nature from the Virgin Mother,
so that same human nature may come to our aid
as we offer to you the sacrifice of thanksgiving.
We ask this through Christ our Lord.

Eucharistic Preface

It is truly right and just, our duty and our salvation,
always and everywhere to give you thanks,
Lord, holy Father, almighty and eternal God.

We celebrate this radiant birthday,
when, like a bright star appearing,
Mary, the Mother of God, was born into the world.
You honoured her with the fullness of grace,
so that through her Son
a new and heavenly birth might be ours
in which death itself should die
and eternal life be given us.

And so, with angels and all saints,
we glorify your holy name: Holy . . .

Prayer after Communion

Let this holy feast which we have shared, O God,
make us open to you,
just as Mary placed herself at the disposal of the One who was to be born of her:
Christ Jesus, the Lord for ever and ever.

14 September Holy Cross Day – Festival

The origin of this feast lies in the dedication day of the Emperor Constantine's basilica complex of the Martyrium and Anastasis in Jerusalem (the site of which is now occupied by the Church of the Holy Sepulchre), which housed the relics of the True Cross. After the recovery of these relics from Persia in the seventh century, the feast spread to the Western churches. The Cross is celebrated today as the Tree of Life, a sign of Christ's humiliation and glory.

Scripture-related opening prayer

God, our deliverer,
you have planted the sign of the cross
as the life-giving tree at the heart of your Church.
Lift up our eyes to the crucified One
who was lifted up for our healing,
that in Christ we may recognize that love
with which you so loved the world.
We ask this through your Son, Jesus the Christ,
who is one with you and the Holy Spirit,
for ever and ever.

Opening prayer

All-powerful God,
who gave your only-begotten Son
to suffer and give his life upon the cross
for the salvation of the human race;
grant that as through baptism we are planted in his death
so we may share the triumph of his risen life in heaven.
We ask this through Jesus Christ our Lord.

Acclamation

John 3:16
V/. God so loved the world that he gave his only Son:
so that everyone who believes in him may have eternal life.

Intercession

God, who in your gracious mercy
redeemed us by the precious blood of your Son;
grant, we pray, that we who reverence his cross
may be set free from the entanglements of our sins.
We ask this through Jesus Christ our Lord.

Prayer over the Gifts

Upon the altar of the cross, O God,
your beloved Son offered his life
to restore our communion with you.
Grant that, as in your providence
you make that altar into a holy table for us,
so may we eat and drink in thanksgiving
for the great love wherewith you have redeemed the world.
We ask this through Christ our Lord.

Eucharistic Preface

It is truly right and just, our duty and our salvation,
always and everywhere to give you thanks,
Lord, holy Father, almighty and eternal God,
through Jesus Christ our Lord.

We celebrate with songs of praise
the cross, the victory-sign of Christ.
Once through the fruit of the forbidden tree, we fell;
now through the tree of the cross
Christ has cancelled the former curse
by becoming accursed for our sake,

to snatch us from our ancient foe
and lead us from death's dominion
into resurrection and eternal life.

And so, for all your wonderful works
we praise you with angels and saints
in their exultant holy hymn: Holy . . .

Prayer after Communion

Nourished at your heavenly table
we beg you, Lord Jesus Christ:
lead to the glory of the resurrection
all whose salvation you purchased
by the life-bestowing wood of the cross,
for you live and reign for ever and ever.

21 September Saint Matthew, Apostle and Evangelist – Festival

Matthew, known as Levi, was a tax collector of Capernaum. Jesus called him to be a disciple. Matthew is venerated as the author of the Gospel, which portrays Jesus as Messianic Teacher of the kingdom of God in five great collections of teaching or 'sermons'.

Scripture-related opening prayer

God, source of all truth,
by whose gracious will
Saint Matthew became a follower of Christ
and exchanged the profits of his tax collecting
for the enduring riches of your wisdom;
give us the courage
to proclaim that same gospel which he made known,
so that, as ministers of your word,

we also may discover true wealth in your kingdom.
We ask this through Jesus Christ,
who is one with you and the Holy Spirit,
for ever and ever.

Opening prayer

Lord our God,
in faithful witness to your Son,
Saint Matthew has given us the gospel of salvation.
From this enduring word,
let your Church draw abundant life,
and grow in union with Christ, the head.
We ask this in the name of Jesus,
our Teacher and Redeemer,
for ever and ever.

Acclamation

Proverbs 3:13–14
V/. Happy are those who find wisdom:
for she is better than silver, richer than gold.

Intercession

Lord God,
let the Christian people rejoice
that in Christ's body we are members one of another;
and let our prayer lead the whole Church
to share in the glory of your holy apostles.
Through Christ our Lord.

Prayer over the Gifts

Generous God,
whose table is prepared for us,
we ask you, that as your Son was pleased

to be a guest in Matthew's house,
so Christ may make this gathering
a place of reconciliation and peace,
to your glory, for ever and ever.

Eucharistic Preface

It is truly right and just, our duty and our salvation,
always and everywhere to give you thanks,
Lord, holy Father, almighty and eternal God.

In Christ your Son
you reveal your compassion for humankind
and in mercy you invite sinners
to sit at the banquet of your kingdom.
Saint Matthew responded to the call of Christ
and made him welcome in his house.
Changed and renewed by the coming of the Lord
he dedicated himself to proclaim
your wonderful works of salvation.

To his preaching of the gospel
we respond with gladness,
joining all the powers of heaven
in this, their unending hymn of praise: Holy . . .

Prayer after Communion

O God, who make us partakers in that same joy
with which Saint Matthew welcomed the Saviour,
nourish us with the food of Christ,
who came to call, not the righteous, but sinners.
We ask this in his name,
our Teacher and Redeemer, for ever and ever.

29 September Saint Michael and All Angels – Festival

In Scripture, angels are messengers of God, created visible beings who do the will of the invisible One. The cult of angels and archangels arose in the Eastern churches. This day was originally the dedication day of a church dedicated to Saint Michael in Rome.

Scripture-related opening prayer

Holy God,
whose awesome presence none can see,
through the ministry of angels and archangels
you come to us with tender care
and strong protection.
Teach us to praise you along with them,
and to be the messengers of your gracious love.
We ask this in the name of Jesus Christ,
who is one with you and the Holy Spirit,
for ever and ever.

Opening prayer

Who is like you, O God?
You are the source of healing and salvation;
you have conquered the powers of evil;
you walk with your people
throughout this earthly pilgrimage.
As we give thanks for Michael,
for archangels, angels and all heavenly powers,
let us know that in them
you stand by us and encourage us,
until that day when we shall see you face to face.
We make this prayer through Christ our Lord.

Acclamation

Prayer of Azariah 37
V/. Bless the Lord, you angels of the Lord:
sing praise to him and highly exalt him for ever.

Intercession

Grant to us, Lord,
the unfailing support of your mercy
which you have ordained
through the ministry of the angels.
We ask this through Christ our Lord.

Prayer over the Gifts

As your angels minister before you, O God,
so we have prepared this table
to celebrate your glory.
Let the gift imparted here
bring us to share that glory
for ever and ever.

Eucharistic Preface

We lift up our hearts to you,
the God and Father of all;
to you we offer thanks and praise,
through Jesus Christ your Son.

As the glorious Master of the universe,
you give life by your word to bodiless creatures,
to whom you allot the joyful ministry
of standing before your throne of majesty.
When the rebellious spirits were cast down,
the host of angels and archangels
became your eternal crown of praise,

while carrying into your presence
our acts of worship, faith and prayer.

And so, with all the angels
we glorify your holy name: Holy . . .

Prayer after Communion

Restored by the bread of heaven
we ask you, Lord,
that in the strength of this food
we may walk in the way of salvation
under the faithful care of your angels.
We make this prayer through Jesus Christ our Lord.

18 October Saint Luke, Evangelist – Festival

Ancient Christian tradition names Saint Luke the Physician as the author of both the third Gospel and the Book of Acts. Luke was a gentile convert and perhaps a companion of Saint Paul. Luke's gospel is a gospel of both compassion and complete surrender to the work of the kingdom.

Scripture-related opening prayer

O God, healer of broken hearts
and courage for the fearful,
who by the witness of Saint Luke
revealed the closeness of your rule;
inspire your people with the Holy Spirit,
that they may proclaim your word with boldness
and reveal your kingdom with deeds of power,
as they wait with longing for the appearing
of the glorious day of Christ,
who is one with you and the Holy Spirit
for ever and ever.

Opening prayer

Lord our God,
you chose Saint Luke
to reveal by his preaching and writing
your steadfast love for the poor.
Grant that those who now rejoice in your name
may continue to be of one heart and mind
and that all peoples may behold your salvation.
This we ask through Christ our Lord.

Acclamation

Psalm 147:3
V/. He heals the brokenhearted:
and binds up all their wounds.

Intercession

You, O God, are the champion
of the poor, of those who lack a voice,
of all who have no other help but you.
As we remember them in prayer,
let your gospel impel us to listen to them,
and be their advocates in time of need.
We ask this through Christ, our Lord.

Prayer over the Gifts

Lord God, we gather at your table.
Open our mouths in your praise,
set our hearts free for your service,
heal what is sick in us
and bring us to your glory.
Through Jesus Christ our Lord.

Eucharistic Preface

It is truly right and just, our duty and our salvation,
always and everywhere to give you thanks,
Lord, holy Father, almighty and eternal God,
through Jesus Christ our Lord.

You willed that the mystery of Christ your Son
should be made known to us through Scriptures,
the work of those you enlightened by the Holy Spirit.
They have entrusted to your Church
the words and acts of the Saviour
in writings that will endure
to be a fertile seed for all generations,
bearing rich fruit to your praise and glory.

And so, with angels and saints,
we sing the ageless hymn of your praise: Holy . . .

Prayer after Communion

Almighty God,
let your holy gift make us holy,
and establish us in the faith of the gospel
which Saint Luke proclaimed.
We ask this through Christ our Lord.

28 October Saint Simon and Saint Jude, Apostles – Festival

Simon is also known as 'the Zealot'. Jude, 'Son of James' (Luke 6:16, Acts 1:13), was traditionally thought to be the same person as Jude, brother of James and author of the New Testament letter. He may be the one named as 'Thaddeus' (Matthew 10:3 and Mark 3:18). Tradition has it that both preached the gospel and were martyred in Persia, where an ancient form of eucharistic liturgy bears the name of 'Addai' (Thaddeus).

Opening prayers

The collect from the Book of Common Prayer, *modernized in* Common Worship, *is based so well on the readings for today that it would be inopportune to try to better it as a Scripture-related opening prayer. However, I have included here two opening prayers from other sources.*

Faithful God,
you chose Simon and Jude to be apostles,
to form the foundation of your Church.
Keep us faithful to their word and example
that we may be living stones,
a consecrated people in Christ,
who is one with you and the Holy Spirit,
for ever and ever.

or:
God, our wisdom,
through the Apostles Simon and Jude
you brought us to recognize your name.
Grant that your Church may grow
and the number of those who believe in you be increased.
We ask this through Jesus Christ our Lord.

Acclamation

cf. Te Deum Laudamus v. 7
V/. The glorious company of the apostles:
praises you for ever, O God.

Intercession

Lord our God,
in the apostles whom Jesus gathered round him,
you showed us what the Church might truly be.
Strengthen our union with them,
so that, united with one another,

we may be a faithful image
of that first community of believers.
We ask this through Jesus Christ the Lord.

Prayer over the Gifts

Lord,
each year we recall the glory
of your holy Apostles Simon and Jude.
Accept our praises this day
in this, the Supper of the Lord,
that we may become one
in the fellowship of all your saints.
We ask this through Christ, our Lord.

Eucharistic Preface

It is truly right and just, our duty and our salvation,
always and everywhere to give you thanks,
Lord, holy Father, almighty and eternal God.

You are the eternal Shepherd
who never leave your flock untended;
but through the holy apostles
you keep it under your continual protection,
so that your people may always be led by those
called by Christ to share his ministry
of shepherd at your Church's head.

Therefore, with angels and saints,
we glorify your holy name: Holy . . .

Prayer after Communion

Gracious God,
we pray in the Holy Spirit
that this celebration to honour the martyrdom

of the Apostles Simon and Jude
may keep us steadfast in your love.
This we ask through Christ our Lord.

1 November All Saints' Day – Principal Feast

The texts for this day are found in the Sunday propers, pp. 132–5.

2 November All Souls' Day – Lesser Festival

The commemoration of all Christian dead began as a sort of 'after-feast' of All Saints' Day. It reflects the natural human desire to commend those who have died to the love of God, not out of fear but in the faith of Christ risen. Prayer and commemoration of the dead imply no particular eschatology, but stem from the resurrection of Jesus and the conviction that he is the first fruits, in whose harvest we shall all be gathered.

Opening prayers

God, who make all things new,
you promise to those who are faithful
a reward for their labours,
and to those who die in Christ
you pledge an eternal blessing.
Let this be our true faith,
so that in life and in death
we may know that nothing can part us
from your eternal love.
We ask this through Christ our Lord.

or:
God of the spirits of all flesh,
let the memory of those who have gone before us
be held and cherished

eternally in your presence,
that no one who belongs to you
may be forgotten.
We ask this through Christ our Lord.

Intercession

God, our shelter and strength,
you listen in love to the cry of your people.
Hear us as we remember those
who have gone before us in faith,
and grant us, with them
the fullness of redemption.
We ask this through Christ our Lord.

Prayer over the Gifts

From your table, O God,
neither life nor death can shut us out.
So let this holy feast be for us
the pledge of things to come,
the bread of tomorrow
and the new wine of your kingdom.
We ask this through Christ our Lord.

Eucharistic Preface
We lift up our hearts to you,
God eternal, true and faithful;
to you we offer thanks and praise
in the name of Jesus Christ.

As the Incarnate Word
he came to live in lowly form amongst us.
As the Immortal One, he assumed our mortality
to suffer on the cross and be laid in the tomb.
But with great power he is risen from the dead,
so that he might raise us together with himself

and clothe our corruptible nature
with the incorruption of eternal life.

And so, in the sure and certain hope
of blessings and wonders to come,
we join the angels and saints
in their new song of everlasting praise: Holy . . .

Prayer after Communion

Merciful God,
let this Communion be strength in weakness,
support in good works,
and for the living and the dead
may it pledge your eternal care
and the glorious inheritance of your saints.
Through Christ our Lord.

PART SEVEN

LITURGIES FOR THE SEASONS BETWEEN EPIPHANY TO LENT AND PENTECOST TO ADVENT

This section provides outlines for services that might be celebrated either as parish celebrations or by smaller groups. The two major feasts of All Saints and The Presentation (Candlemas) have a pivotal role in the *Common Worship* annual cycle. All Saints marks the transition from the 'ordinary' Sundays to the pre-Advent or 'Kingdom' season, while the feast of the Presentation of the Lord marks the end of the Epiphany season.

It might be thought appropriate to mark these occasions with a vigil service, as a preparation for the feast. The vigil might take the place of Evening Prayer on the eve.

In addition, this section offers a form for prayer in commemoration of the dead, a short service that may be held in the church or in a cemetery chapel.

Thirdly, a form is given for a parish or group service for the sick, which contains a celebration of the Laying on of Hands and Anointing of the Sick.

I. Services for All Saints' Day, All Souls' Day and the Presentation of the Lord (Candlemas)

Two sets of outlines for Vigil services are given in this section: for All Saints and Candlemas. They reflect the tradition of liturgical Vigil as found in the monastic and breviary traditions.

It is envisaged that the Vigil, being held in the evening, would replace Evening Prayer. It might begin with a ceremony of light. The two alternatives offered here for Services of Light may be used with the orders given for Vigils of All Saints and Candlemas.

The principal part of a Vigil is the speaking of the Word of God, and the opportunity given to the participants to listen and reflect.

The readings may be spoken by several readers, balancing male and female voices as appropriate. Each reading might be divided into shorter pieces interspersed by silence. It is important to use creativity and imagination in the presentation of the Scriptures at a Vigil.

Periods of silence are recommended.

Congregations unfamiliar with silence in worship might be encouraged to engage with the Scriptures by, for example, allowing words or phrases from the readings to surface in their minds and quietly repeating them over again to themselves.

Alternatively, people might be encouraged to bring a Bible, NOT to follow the reading in it, but afterwards to look back over the text and try to absorb it themselves.

Responsories, that is, collections of Scripture or psalm verses juxtaposed, may be used to illuminate the meaning of the Scriptures. Some are suggested below, attached to the suggested readings.

Other ways of illuminating the Word of God might be considered, such as mime and dance.

The space between readings should be generous.

First Service of Light

The person leading the service greets the people in these words:

Leader: In the name of our Lord Jesus Christ, light and peace be with you all.
All: And also with you.

Candles are lit in whatever way is appropriate to provide light to read the scriptures by and to see each other clearly. A song or hymn may be sung, for example:

O gladsome Light (New English Hymnal 247)
Holy Father, cheer our way (New English Hymnal 246)
Lighten our darkness (Hymns for Today's Church 278)
O radiant Light (Gather 9)
I am the Light of the world (Gather 510)

When the candles are lit, this prayer is said by the leader.

Opening prayer

God our Father,
you glorify in your kingdom
those servants found faithful
and watching in the night.
As we keep vigil,
keep alight in our hands
the lamp of your love,
that we may enter
into the hall of your eternal banquet,
where you reign for ever and ever.
All: Amen.

or:

We praise you,
God of light and glory;

for as daylight fades
you will not let the darkness cover us.
From your radiance
we kindle a light
by which to speak and hear your word.
As we listen,
we pray you to kindle in our heart
the light of love and faith.
Lead us by that unfailing light
to the place where you desire us to be,
the new and eternal Jerusalem
where with all your saints
we are to enjoy your beauty and glory
for ever and ever. *All:* Amen.

Second Service of Light

The leader begins the service:

Leader: Christ is the light of the world:
All: a light that shines in the darkness.
Leader: Awake, sleeper, and arise from the dead:
All: and Christ shall be your light.

Two people from those gathered bring forward lights. One of them recites these words:

With our sacred lights we bring our hopes
that you will enkindle in us
the fire of your love,
to fill the hearts of your people
and renew the face of the earth.

Two more people come forward with lights.

With these bright lights we bring our prayers
that you will enlighten our minds
with the radiance of your love,
to scatter the darkness of doubt
and restore our faith in the future.

Two more people come forward with lights.

With solemn lights we bring our desire
that you will drive away the shadow of despair
with the strength of your glory,
and dare us to dream again
of a world at peace in harmony
where the lion may lie down with the lamb.

Two more people come forward with lights.

With sparkling lights we bring our plea
that you will illuminate our pathways ahead
with the guidance of the gospel,
to enrich the quality of our living
and enhance our capacity for loving.

Other lights are provided as appropriate.

A hymn is sung; if a Taizé or Iona refrain is used, it may be integrated with the candle lighting and prayers above.

Prayer

The light of God's word shines within us,
discovering the dark places of our sinfulness
and strengthening what is good within us.
R/. Blessed be God for ever.

The light of God's word shines through history
displacing darkness, awakening life
and arousing hope in God's eternal purpose.
R/. Blessed be God for ever.

The light of the presence of Jesus Christ
is radiant with joy and merciful judgement,
for Christ is the light of life.
R/. Blessed be God for ever.

Suggested Vigil Readings, Responses and Prayers for All Saints

First reading: Genesis 12:1–8

Abram, our ancestor in faith, is called by God

Response to the reading: Psalm 105:1–15

or:

Responsory

Genesis 12:2, 3; Luke 9:23
R/. Go from your country and your kindred and your father's house to the land that I will show you. In you all the families of the earth shall be blessed.
V/. If any want to become my followers, let them deny themselves and take up their cross daily and follow me:
R/. In you all the families of the earth shall be blessed.

Psalm prayer

O God of Abraham, Isaac and Jacob,
you redeemed us from the slavery of sin
for freedom as your children:
feed us on our way with the bread of heaven
and quench our thirst with living water;
through Christ our Lord.

or:
God of our pilgrimage,
you summoned Abram
to follow you in ways he did not know
and put his faith in things he could not see.
Bless all who honour him as their ancestor
and draw them together in understanding
and reverence for your name.
We ask this through Christ our Lord.

Second reading: Daniel 3:1–30 (careful abridgement may be desired)

The Angel of God saves the three young men in the furnace

Response to the reading: The Song of the Three 29–34

or:

Responsory

Daniel 3:28; 4:3

R/. Blessed be God, who has sent his angel and delivered his servants who trusted in him. For there is no other god who is able to deliver in this way.
V/. How great are his signs, how mighty his wonders. His kingdom is an everlasting kingdom.
R/. For there is no other god who is able to deliver in this way.

Prayer

God most blessed,
dwelling on high,
scanning the depths,
let your angel stand beside us,
your strong hand shield us
and your word be our guide,
through Jesus Christ our Lord.

Third reading: Sirach 44:1–15

The praises due to the heroes of old

Response to the reading: Psalm 112

or:

Responsory

Sirach 44:1; Psalm 112:6

R/. Let us now sing the praises of famous men, our ancestors in their generations. The Lord apportioned to them great glory, his majesty from the beginning.
V/. For they will never be shaken, the righteous will be kept in everlasting remembrance.
R/. The Lord apportioned to them great glory, his majesty from the beginning.

Psalm prayer

God, the fountain of all holiness,
you blessed your saints on earth
with many different gifts of grace
and in heaven you fulfil them
with the one reward of glory.
Grant that each of us in our vocation

may lead a life worthy of our calling.
We ask this through Christ our Lord.

Fourth reading: Hebrews 11:32—12:3

The great cloud of witnesses that surrounds us

Response to the reading: Canticle of Ephesians, Ephesians 1:3–10

or:

Responsory

Hebrews 12:1,2; Ephesians 1:2
R/. Let us lay aside every weight and run with perseverance the race that is set before us; Looking to Jesus the pioneer and perfecter of our faith.
V/. God chose us before the foundation of the world, that we should be holy and blameless before him:
R/. Looking to Jesus the pioneer and perfecter of our faith.

Prayer

All your works give you praise, O God,
and your faithful servants bless you.
To us you give an inheritance with them
in your everlasting reign;
so give us also the will
to make known the glory of your kingdom.
We ask this through Christ our Lord.

Fifth reading: Revelation 7:1–17

The vision of a great multitude that none could count

Response to the reading: Canticle, Revelation 21:1–5a

or:

Responsory

cf. Revelation 11:16–18
R/. We give you thanks, Lord God almighty, who are and who were: for you have taken your great power and begun to reign.
V/. The time has come for rewarding your servants, the prophets and saints and all who fear your name both small and great:
R/. For you have taken your great power and begun to reign.

Prayer

Eternal God,
before whom stand men and women
from all times, all nations and all tongues,
grant us the courage
to accept your rule
that we may enter the glory
of your eternal kingdom.
We ask this through Christ our Lord.

Gospel reading

The Gospel is then proclaimed. A hymn suitable to the occasion may precede the Gospel, or a Gospel Acclamation with Alleluia, such as:

Romans 8:16
V/. The Spirit bears witness with our spirit:
that we are the children of God.

The Gospel may be either

Matthew 5:1–12 (The Beatitudes) or
Luke 18:18–30 (How to inherit eternal life).

A sermon or homily may be given.

The Vigil ends with either

the Canticle Te Deum Laudamus *and the Collect for All Saints' Day*
or, if the Vigil replaces Evening Prayer, the Canticle Magnificat *and the Collect for All Saints' Day.*

A Service of Commemoration of the Departed

These days, the coming of 'Hallowe'en' is often the occasion for fun; however, many Christians discern a current of paganism or superstition or simple 'spookiness' in the way many people observe this day. In itself this is probably not harmful, but the Church has always tried to keep celebrations like this focused on the risen Christ.

It is good to encourage people to remember their dead. However, this should not be understood as if the dead were in any other place than in the hands of God, as a harvest whose 'first fruits' is the risen Christ (1 Corinthians 15:23).

This service is based on that used for several years now in the author's own parish community.

This service is intended to gather people either in church or at a cemetery chapel to pray in commemoration of the departed. It is appropriate to hold it on All Souls' Day, or in the evening of All Saints' Day.

Welcome

The leader greets the gathering:

V/. Blessed be God, Father, Son and Holy Spirit.
R/. And blessed be the kingdom, now and for ever.

The leader invites people to come to a candle stand and light a candle, speaking aloud the name of those they wish to remember in this service. While this is being done, a suitable song may be sung, such as:

Listen, Lord (Iona)
Stay with me (Taizé)
Jesus remember me (Taizé)
Grant them eternal rest O Lord (Laudate 439)

When all have lighted their candles, the leader says: Let us pray.

Silence is kept for a while.

Prayer

God of unchanging light,
whose wisdom has created all things new;
remember those who have died,
those known and loved by us
and those unknown.
Shine upon them
and transform the shadows of death
into the glorious light of the resurrection,
in Christ, Jesus your Son,
who is one with you and the Holy Spirit,
for ever and ever.

Ministry of the Word

Reading: 1 John 3:1–3

The children of God

Responsorial Psalm 91

R/. God's angel will keep me in safety;
no evil shall I fear.

The reading and psalm are followed by a time of silence and remembrance.

Intercession

A bowl for burning incense is placed before the congregation. The leader invites people to come and place a grain of incense on the coals. While people are doing this, the Taizé chant O Lord hear my prayer *is sung. This may be used as a refrain with verses from either Psalm 141 or 130.*

Leader:
Let us pray to Christ, the risen One,
our life and resurrection.
A sung response such as Kyrie eleison *is recommended. There are plainsong, Taizé and Iona versions of this.*

You raised Lazarus from the dead;
grant life to all who have died in faith.
R/.

You restored her son to the widow of Nain;
comfort all who mourn their dead.
R/.

By your passion, you took away the power of sin;
destroy the powers that oppress men and women.
R/.

You gave sight to the man born blind;
open the eyes of the dead to your glory.
R/.

You have given us the vision of resurrection;
make our mortal body like yours in glory.
R/.

You promise an eternal dwelling place;
remember us, when our earthly dwelling is ended.
R/.

Remember us, Lord, in your kingdom,
and teach us to pray:
All: Our Father . . .

Prayer

In your sight, O God,
our prayer rises like incense.
Let the memory of those who have died
come before you and find your welcome,
that they may live anew in Christ your Son,
who lives and reigns for ever and ever.

If the service is taking place in a church with a burial ground or a local cemetery chapel, it would be appropriate for the congregation to go in procession around this area or a part of it. In many Christian cultures, it is customary to light votive lamps on the graves and to decorate them with flowers.

The service ends with a sign of peace. The leader says:

Leader: The peace of Christ be always with us;
All: Peace for the living, peace for the departed.
Leader: Let us offer each other a sign of Christ's peace.

All exchange a sign of peace together.

Readings for the Vigil of the Presentation of Christ in the Temple Candlemas

This feast originated in Jerusalem before the fifth century and was adopted in Rome during the seventh century. In the annual cycle as set out in Common Worship, *it marks the formal end of the Christmas period. On such an occasion a Vigil is appropriate. This Vigil may take place on the evening of 1 February.*

In place of one of the alternatives for the Service of Light given above, the rite of blessing and procession with lighted candles *(see pp. 16–17)* *may begin the Vigil. If this is the option chosen, the procession will conclude with the Collect, which will be followed by the readings.*

First reading: Exodus 13:1, 2, 11–16

God commands the consecration of all the firstborn

Response to the reading: Psalm 66:1–11

or:

Responsory

Psalm 116:15, 16; Exodus 13:2
R/. I will offer you the sacrifice of thanksgiving and call upon the name of the Lord. I will fulfil my vows to the Lord in the presence of all his people.
V/. Consecrate to me all the firstborn; whatever is the first to open the womb is mine:
R/. I will fulfil my vows to the Lord in the presence of all his people.

Prayer

Faithful God,
keep alive in us the memory
of the wonderful deeds
that brought us salvation,
that we may fulfil our vows to you
and call on your holy name.
We ask this through Christ our Lord.

Second reading: Isaiah 6:1–8

The holiness of the Lord fills the sanctuary

Response to the reading: Psalm 99

or

Responsory

Isaiah 6:1, 2; Revelation 4:8
R/. I saw the Lord sitting on a throne, high and lofty, and the Seraphs called out one to the other and said: Holy, Holy, Holy is the Lord of Hosts, the whole earth is full of his glory.
V/. The four living creatures, each of them with six wings, are full of eyes all round and inside, and day and night without ceasing they sing:
R/. Holy, Holy, Holy is the Lord of hosts, the whole earth is full of his glory.

Prayer

God most high,
you stoop to embrace our lowliness
and call us to be holy as you are holy
Direct our lives in righteousness
so that our worship may give you glory.
We ask this through Christ our Lord.

Third reading: Haggai 2:1–9

God promises that his splendour shall fill the Temple

Response to the reading: Psalm 24

or:

Responsory

Ezkekiel 43:4; Luke 2:22
R/. The glory of the Lord entered the Temple by the gate facing east; and the glory of the Lord filled the Temple.
V/. The parents of Jesus brought him to Jerusalem to present him to the Lord:
R/. And the glory of the Lord filled the Temple.

Prayer

God of blessings,
purify our hearts
by your Holy Spirit
and make us a temple for your glory.
We ask this through Christ our Lord.

Fourth reading: 1 John 1:1–10

God is light, and in him is no darkness at all

Response to the reading: Psalm 139:1–11

or

Responsory

John 1:14, 16; 1 John 1:1)
R/. We saw his glory, the glory as of the Father's only Son, full of grace and truth. From his fullness we have all received, grace upon grace.
V/. We declare to you what was from the beginning, concerning the word of life. This life was revealed and we have seen it.
R/. From his fullness we have all received, grace upon grace.

Prayer

Almighty and eternal God,
through the coming of your only-begotten Son
you shed upon us a new and radiant light.
Grant that, as through his birth of the Virgin Mary,
he has come as one like us,
so we may share new life with him
in the kingdom of his grace.
We ask this through Christ our Lord.

Fifth reading: Revelation 21:1–27 (abridgement may be appropriate)

The temple of the city is the Lord God and the Lamb

Response to the reading: Psalm 46

or:

Responsory

Revelation 21:22, 23, 26
R/. The city has no need of sun or moon to shine on it, for the glory of God is its light, and its lamp is the Lamb. People will bring into it the glory and the honour of the nations.
V/. I saw no temple in the city, for its temple is the Lord God the Almighty and the Lamb.
R/. People will bring into it the glory and the honour of the nations.

Prayer

Christ, our true temple,
in whose body we are made one;
fill us with that light
which is the gift of the Holy Spirit,
and let our lives and actions

be illuminated by your grace,
now and for ever.

Gospel reading

The Gospel is then proclaimed. A hymn suitable to the occasion may precede the Gospel, or a Gospel Acclamation with Alleluia, such as:

Luke 2:32
V/. The light for revelation to the Gentiles:
and for glory to your people Israel.

Gospel: Luke 2:22–40.

A sermon or homily may be given.

The Vigil ends with the Canticle Te Deum Laudamus *and the Collect for the Presentation. If the Vigil began with the Procession, the alternative Collect, pp. 17–18 should be used.*

If the Vigil replaces Evening Prayer, it may end with the Canticle Magnificat *instead of the* Te Deum, *followed by the Collect for the Presentation. If the Vigil began with the Procession, the alternative Collect, pp. 17–18 should be used.*

11. A Service for the Sick with Anointing

The time around Saint Luke's Day (18 October) is often used as a time of prayer for the sick and those who care for the sick. The service outlined here might be appropriate for Saint Luke's Tide or at other times.

Healing was central to the ministry of Jesus Christ. In the Gospels it is a sign of the coming reign of God. Jesus sent out disciples with the command to preach and to heal. Saint Mark records that they anointed the sick with oil.

Just as men and women asked the Lord for healing, so today those who are sick may ask for the ministry of the Church in the form of prayer or the laying on of hands or anointing. This request is in itself significant as a sign of that faith which, according to Christ, is crucial in their healing and reconciliation.

For many, sickness takes on a less obvious form in the shape of depression, anxiety or simple exhaustion. This may be physical, but it can be spiritual too. The Christian understanding of 'soul' is that it encompasses desire, understanding, will and imagination. For many, there may be unhealed and damaged parts of the soul. For all sickness, the ministry of Jesus was one of healing and forgiveness.

Sickness is for many a time of absence from the community, sometimes of isolation and loneliness, so it might be particularly significant to gather the sick of the community to pray together with their fellow believers and carers. This service might also be held in a hospital chapel for a number of patients and staff.

This service, or parts of it, might be used as an alternative to the provisions contained in *Common Worship, Ministry to the Sick* (Church House Publishing 2000, p. 82).

If the oil to be used has been blessed previously, the prayer of blessing is not used and the shorter blessing over the oil is used instead. In Anglican communities, the minister who anoints must be authorized for this ministry as required by Canon B 37.

If this service is to take place at a celebration of the Eucharist, the prayer for the sick takes the place of the Intercession. The Preparation of the Table follows the Anointing and the Eucharist continues as usual.

Welcome

The service may open with a hymn or gathering song of praise, such as:

God is love (New English Hymnal 364)
Love divine (New English Hymnal 408)
Through all the changing scenes of life (New English Hymnal 467)
Praise him (Hymns for Today's Church 25)
Tell out, my soul (Hymns for Today's Church 42)
Bring to the Lord a glad new song (Hymns for Today's Church 336)

The leader greets the gathering in the name of Christ:

Leader: From the risen One, Christ the healer of souls,
grace and peace be with you all.
All: And also with you.

The leader, or another minister, may briefly welcome everyone and introduce the service. He might use words such as these:

Introduction

Dear friends in Christ,
we have gathered in his name
to celebrate his presence among us
as the physician of souls.

In the Gospels we learn
that the sick came to him and were healed.

Indeed, so great was his love for us
that he took our weakness on himself
and suffered death for our sake.

Through the Apostle James he has commanded
that the elders of the Church lay hands on the sick
and anoint them with oil in his name.

Let our celebration today
give new heart to all
who are troubled in body or spirit.
In the silence of our hearts
let us commend them to Christ
and to his tender care.

All pray in silence for a few moments.

One of these collects may be used:

Collect
Almighty God,
who chose that your only-begotten Son
should bear our infirmities
to display your power to save,
graciously hear us as we pray,
that all who are weighed down
by pain, distress or disease
may know that they are counted among the elect
whom Christ has called blessed,
and that they are united with his suffering
for the salvation of the world.
We ask this through Jesus Christ our Lord.

or:

Loving God,
in whom all things are made whole,

you sent your Son our Saviour
to heal a broken world.
Visit us with your salvation,
that we may be blessed
in body, mind and spirit;
through Jesus Christ our Lord.

or:

O God of peace,
you have taught us
that in returning and rest we shall be saved,
in quietness and confidence shall be our strength:
by the might of your Spirit
lift us, we pray, to your presence
where we may be still and know that you are God;
through Jesus Christ our Lord.

Ministry of the Word

One or more readings are spoken. If only one reading is to be used, the Gospel reading should be preferred.

Readings from the Old Testament

Isaiah 35:1–10
Strengthen the weak hands
Response: Psalm 123

or:

Isaiah 61:1–4
The Spirit of the Lord, the Consoler
Response: Psalm 143

Readings from the New Testament

Romans 8:18–27
We groan while we await the redemption of our bodies
Response: Psalm 30

or:

2 Corinthians 4:16–18
The inner nature is being renewed day by day
Response: Psalm 27:7–14

or:

James 5:13–16
The prayer of faith will save the sick person
Response: Psalm 40:13–17

The Gospel

Gospel Acclamation to be sung with Alleluia: *Matthew 8:17*
V/. Christ took our sicknesses away:
and carried our diseases for us.

Matthew 8:5–17
He took our sickness away

or:

Acclamation: Matthew 11:28
V/. 'Come to me, all you that are weary:
and I will give you rest,' says the Lord.

Matthew 11:25–30
You will find rest for your souls

or:

Acclamation: Mark 2:12
V/. The man stood up and took up his mat and went out:
and they were all amazed and glorified God.

Mark 2:1–12
The healing of the paralysed man

or:

Acclamation: Mark 4:41
V/. They said: 'Who can this be?
Even the winds and the sea obey him.'

Mark 4:35–41
The Lord calms the storm

or:

Acclamation: Luke 4:18
V/. The Spirit of the Lord is upon me:
for he has anointed me.

Luke 4:16–21
Jesus is anointed to proclaim the year of God's favour

or:

Acclamation: Matthew 8:17
V/. Christ took our sicknesses away:
and carried our diseases for us.

Luke 10:5–9
The disciples are sent out

or:

Acclamation: Matthew 8:17
Christ took our sicknesses away:
and carried our diseases for us.

Luke 10:25–37
Who is my neighbour?

After the Gospel, there may be an address.

Prayer, Laying on of Hands and Anointing form the core of the Church's ministry to the sick, as set out in the Letter of Saint James (5:13–16).

Prayer

Prayer form 1

Leader :
The sick and suffering came to Christ in faith
and he responded to their faith
in compassion and healing.
Confident in his goodness
we now bring before him
those who need his healing touch.
So we pray:
Lord Jesus Christ, lover of all:
All: Give us your peace.

We name before you
those who are ill in body:
whose illness is long or painful
or difficult to cure;
who suffer restless days
and sleepless nights.

Pause for silent prayer

Lord Jesus Christ, lover of all:
All: Give us your peace.

We name before you
those who are troubled in mind,
distressed by the past
or dreading the future;
those who are trapped
and cast down by fear.

Pause for silent prayer

Lord Jesus Christ, lover of all:
All: Give us your peace.

We name before you
those for whom light has been turned to darkness:
by the death of a loved one;
the breaking of a friendship;
the fading of hope.

Pause for silent prayer

Lord Jesus Christ, lover of all:
All: Give us your peace.

In silence we remember before you
those whose names
we cannot speak aloud.

Pause for silent prayer

Lord Jesus Christ, lover of all:
All: Give us your peace.

We ask your blessing
on doctors and nurses;

on all who look after
those who are ill;
who give friendship
to those who are distressed,
or sit with those
who are near to death.

Pause for silent prayer

Lord Jesus Christ, lover of all:
All: Give us your peace.

We ask your guidance
for those who are engaged
in medical research,
that they may persevere
with wisdom and energy;
and for those who administer
the agencies of health and welfare,
that they may have
wisdom and compassion.

Pause for silent prayer

Lord Jesus Christ, lover of all:
All: Give us your peace.

Prayer Form 2

Leader:
Let us offer the prayer of faith
to seek the salvation of all
who have come here to pray with us.

The sick may be named individually.

Another minister may say:
Through prayer and the laying on of hands
and anointing in the name of Christ,
may he give strength and patience
to those who are sick:

All: Lord, hear our prayer.

May Christ the risen One
free them from all harm,
all sin and all temptation:

All: Lord, hear our prayer.

May Christ the Healer
relieve the sufferings
of all who are sick:

All: Lord, hear our prayer.

May Christ the Good Samaritan
empower and assist all those
dedicated to the care of the sick:

All: Lord, hear our prayer.

May Christ, the creating hands of God,
renew the spirit of his sons and daughters
on whom we lay our hands in his name:

All: Lord, hear our prayer.

Laying on of Hands

The laying on of hands may be done in silence, with all praying quietly. If there are many sick, it would be appropriate to sing a hymn at this point, such as:

Lay your hands gently upon us (*Laudate* 432)

Anointing

If the oil has been blessed already, this prayer of thanksgiving is said over it:
We thank you, God our Father.
You have loved us from the beginning of time
and remembered us when we were in trouble.
All: Blessed be God for ever.

We thank you, Christ the Redeemer.
You humbled yourself to share in our humanity
and you heal our infirmities.
All: Blessed be God for ever.

We thank you, Holy Spirit, Consoler.
You have been poured out upon us,
to comfort us and lead us into all truth.
All: Blessed be God for ever.

God of mercy,
ease the sufferings
and comfort the weakness of your people
whom we anoint with this holy oil.
We ask this through Christ our Lord.
All: Amen.

If the oil is to be blessed, the priest says this prayer:

God of all consolation,
you chose and sent your Son to heal the world.
Graciously listen to our prayer of faith:
send the power of the Holy Spirit, the Consoler,
into this precious oil,
a soothing ointment,
a rich gift,
the fruit of the earth.

Bless this oil and sanctify it for our use.
(the priest may make the sign of the cross over the vessel containing the oil)

Make this oil a remedy for all who are anointed with it;
heal them in body, soul and spirit,
and deliver them from every affliction.

We ask this through our Lord Jesus Christ your Son,
who lives and reigns with you and the Holy Spirit,
one God, for ever and ever.

All: Amen.

The sick are anointed. This may be done on the forehead and palms of the hands. The anointing is accompanied by one of these two sets of words:

Form 1

Through this holy anointing
may Christ in his love and mercy help you
with the grace of the Holy Spirit.
The person anointed says: Amen.

May Christ, who frees you from sin,
save you and raise you up.
Answer: Amen.

or:

Form 2

N,
beloved child of God,
be anointed by Christ
and strengthened by the Holy Spirit
for freedom, for peace
and for eternal life.
Answer: Amen.

When the anointing is finished, the leader calls everyone to pray. Then he or she recites the concluding prayer, changing the gender or number where necessary:

God of all compassion,
give to all those with whom we have prayed
patience in their suffering,
courage amid their fears
and hope when they are dejected.
And when they are alone
let them know the prayers and support
of all your faithful people.
We ask this through Christ our Lord.

Leader:
Let us pray to the Father,
as Christ has taught us, saying:
All: Our Father . . .

Leader:
The grace of our Lord Jesus Christ,
and the love of God, and the fellowship of the Holy Spirit,
be with us all, evermore:
All: Amen.

Epiphany to Lent and Pentecost to Advent

If this service is used in the celebration of the Eucharist, these prayers may be used:

Prayer over the Gifts

Merciful God,
as these gifts of bread and wine
will be for us the gifts of Christ the risen One,
so may he unite our sufferings with his
and cause us to rise to new life.
We ask this through Christ our Lord.

Eucharistic Preface

Father all-holy, it is right to give you thanks,
for in Christ the healer
you reveal your unfailing power
and steadfast compassion.

In the splendour of his resurrection,
your Son conquered suffering and death
and gave us his promise
of a new and glorious world,
where no bodily pain or anguish of soul will afflict us.
Through your gift of the Holy Spirit
you bless us with comfort and healing,
strength and hope, forgiveness and peace.

In this great sacrament of your love,
you feed us on the risen body of your Son:
a pattern of what we shall be
when he returns at the end of time.

And so, with angels and saints,
we glorify your holy name
in this, their ageless hymn of praise: Holy . . .

Prayer after Communion

Gentle God,
through these holy gifts
you offer us the gift of your healing.
May this grace bear fruit among us
and make us strong in your service.
We ask this through Christ our Lord.

SOURCES AND ACKNOWLEDGEMENTS

There are many sources for the texts contained in this book. I have acknowledged below all those who have kindly consented to their material being included, and in some cases modified to suit the context or purpose of the text. To them I offer my thanks.

However, the process of creating texts for worship is complex and any writer will find that they have unconsciously used sources stored in their head, whose exact origin is long forgotten. I am greatly indebted to the tradition of worship, both Anglican and Roman Catholic, in which I have been brought up. Over many years I must have absorbed phrases and images that I cannot now attribute. So should any reader recognize here words, phrases, expressions or patterns of speech that are their own, I would hope that they would understand the difficulty of seeking permission to reproduce what is unconsciously quoted, and also the fact that such unconscious borrowing is a tribute to their work.

If any copyright material is found to have been used here without permission or acknowledgment, this is solely due to the author's inadvertence. He or the publishers will be grateful to be informed and will be pleased to supply the necessary attribution in future editions.

The symbol * in the lists below denotes that the text used has been modified.

All Gospel Acclamations are taken from *The New Revised Standard Version of the Bible* (Anglicized Edition), © 1989,

1995 by the Division of the National Council of Churches of Christ in the United States of America and are used by permission.

Most of the Eucharistic Prefaces are taken from the translations in Alan Griffiths, *We Give You Thanks and Praise, the Eucharistic Prefaces of the Ambrosian Rite* (Canterbury Press 1999).

The sourced prayers are taken by permission from the following:

The Prayer over the Gifts* for Epiphany 3,
The Prayer over the Gifts for Candlemas,
The Intercession* for Proper 19,
The Prayer over the Gifts* for Proper 19,
The Intercession* for Proper 21,
The Prayer over the Gifts* for Proper 23,
The Scripture-related opening prayer* for Proper 5 (continuous series),

are all taken or adapted from *The Book of Alternative Services of the Anglican Church of Canada*, © 1985 by the General Synod of the Anglican Church of Canada (Anglican Book Centre, Toronto, third printing 1986). All rights reserved. Used with permission.

The Scripture-related opening prayer* for Proper 8 (continuous series),
The prayer beginning 'The light of God's word' for the Vigil of All Saints,
The prayer over the people 'God of all' in Part Two, Proper 25,
The Intercession in the Service for the Sick,
The Intercession for Proper 25,

are all taken from *The Book of Common Order of the Church of Scotland* © 1994 *Panel on Worship of the Church of Scotland* (Saint Andrew Press, Edinburgh, 1994). Used with permission.

The Anthems for the Breaking of the Eucharistic Bread, numbers 5, 9*,
The second collect* in the Service for the Sick,
are taken from *The Book of Occasional Services*, ©1979 by the Church Pension Fund (The Church Hymnal Corporation, New York, 1979).

The opening prayer for the Second Sunday of Lent,
The opening prayer for the Sunday before Lent,
The opening prayer for Proper 15,
The Intercession for Proper 18,
The Scripture-related opening prayer* for Proper 20B (continuous series),
The Scripture-related opening prayer* for Proper 22 (continuous series),
The Scripture-related opening prayer for Proper 24B (continuous series),
The Scripture-related opening prayer* for Proper 19C (continuous series),
The Scripture-related opening prayer* for Proper 23C (continuous series),
The 'Song of the Light' in the Sunday Vigil,
The psalm prayer on Psalm 105 in the Vigil of All Saints,
are taken from *Celebrating Common Prayer* (Mowbray), © The Society of Saint Francis 1992. Used with permission.

The Preface for Proper 10C is taken from Alan Griffiths, *Focus on the Eucharistic Prayer* (Kevin Mayhew 1988).

The Intercession* for Proper 25,
The Thanksgiving over the Oil* in the Service for the Sick, (adapted),
are taken from *The Methodist Worship Book*, © 1999 Trustees for Methodist Church Purposes (used by permission of Methodist Publishing House, Peterborough, 1999).

The Prayer over the Gifts for Proper 2,
The opening prayer for Trinity Sunday,
The opening prayer for Proper 6,
The opening prayer for Proper 17,
The alternative Scripture-related opening prayer for Proper 8A (continuous series),
The alternative Scripture-related opening prayer for Proper 13A (continuous series),
The Scripture-related opening prayer for Proper 17A (continuous series),
The Scripture-related opening prayer for Proper 24A (continuous series),
The Scripture-related opening prayer for Proper 7B (continuous series),
The Scripture-related opening prayer for Proper 18B (continuous series),
The Scripture-related opening prayer for Proper 7C (continuous series),
The Scripture-related opening prayer for Proper 21 C (continuous series),
The alternative opening prayer for the Transfiguration,
are taken from Janet Morley, *All Desires Known*, © 1998 Janet Morley (Movement for the Ordination of Women 1988, now administered by SPCK), used by permission.

The Prayer of Light 'O Lord our God . . .' in the Sunday Vigil is taken from *A Book of Prayers translated, edited and published by the Monks of New Skete, Cambridge, New York 12816*, © 1988 Monks of New Skete (New Skete 1988), used by permission.

The Intercession* for Proper 2,
The opening prayer* for Proper 5,
The Eucharistic Preface 'Creation and Redemption',
The Eucharistic Preface 'The Work of God in Christ',
The Prayer after Communion* for the Second Sunday before Advent,

are taken or adapted from Huub Oosterhuis, *Your Word is Near, Contemporary Christian Prayers*, tr. N. D. Smith, © 1968 by the Missionary Society of St. Paul the Apostle in the State of New York (Paulist Press, New York/Ramsey, 1968). Permission sought.

The following texts in the Service for the Sick:
The Oil Blessing*,
The Anointing Formula*,
The Prayer after Anointing*,
are taken or adapted from *Pastoral Care of the Sick, Rites of Anointing and Viaticum*, English translation approved for use in the Dioceses of Ireland, England and Wales, Scotland, © 1982 International Commission on English in the Liturgy (ICEL). All rights reserved. Used by permission.

The Scripture-related opening prayer* for the Baptism of Christ Year A,
The opening prayer* for the Baptism of Christ,
The Intercession for Trinity Sunday,
The Intercession for Proper 9,
The opening prayer* for Proper 10,
The alternative Scripture-related opening prayer* for Proper 11C,
The Intercession for Proper 13,
The opening prayer for Proper 16,
The Prayer over the Gifts* for Proper 17,
The alternative Scripture-related opening prayer* for Proper 21A,
The Intercession* for Corpus Christi,
The Intercession* for the Birth of Saint John the Baptist,
The Intercession* for Saints Peter and Paul,
The Scripture-related opening prayer* for the Transfiguration,
The Intercession* for the Transfiguration,
The Intercession for the Birth of the Blessed Virgin Mary,
The opening prayer* for Saint Matthew,

The Intercession* for the Conversion of Saint Paul,
The Intercession* for Saints Simon and Jude,
The three Prayers of Incense in the Sunday Vigil,
The opening prayer* in the All Saints' Vigil,
are taken from *Proclaiming All Your Wonders, Prayers for a Pilgrim People*, translated from the French *Prières au fil des heures*, Commission francophone cistercienne (Dominican Publications Dublin, 1991). Used by permission.

The Eucharistic Preface 'Christ the Saviour of All' in the numbered Propers is taken from *Masses for the Holy Year 2000*, published and translated by the Committee for the Great Jubilee, Secretariat of State, Vatican City 2000, used by permission.

The Intercession and Prayer after Communion for Saint David are taken from *The Proper of Saints – National Calendar for England and Wales* (The Sacramentary Segment Five bis) (Bishops' Conference of England and Wales 1973 and 1996), used by permission.

The Scripture-related opening prayer* for Candlemas,
The Scripture-related opening prayer* for Proper 2B,
The Scripture-related opening prayer* for Proper 22B,
The Scripture-related opening prayer* for Proper 11C (continuous series),
The Scripture-related opening prayer* for Proper 15C (continuous series),
are reprinted from Peter J. Scagnelli, *Prayers for Sundays and Seasons*, © 1998 Archdiocese of Chicago: Liturgy Training Publications, 1800 North Hermitage Avenue, Chicago, Ill. 60622-1101; 1-800-933-1800, fax 1-800-933-7094, email orders@ltp.org. All rights reserved, used by permission.

The Scripture-related opening prayer* for Proper 20B is based on lines from a eucharistic prayer by David Power, in David Power, OMI, *The Eucharistic Mystery, Revitalizing the Tradition* (Gill and Macmillan, Dublin, 1992). Used by permission.

The Commemoration of the Saints Litany* in the All Saints' Day Procession: Extracts adapted from *The Promise of His Glory*, which is copyright, © The Central Board of Finance of the Church of England, 1991; The Archbishops' Council, 1999.

The Intercession for Epiphany 4,
The Eucharistic Preface* for Proper 3,
The Intercession for Proper 16,
The Intercession* for Proper 20,
The opening prayer* for Proper 21,
The opening prayer* for Proper 22,
The opening prayer* for Proper 25,
The Blessing of Water in the Commemoration of Baptism,
are taken from *The Roman Missal*, © 1973 International Commission on English in the Liturgy (ICEL). All rights reserved. Used by permission.

The hymn books referred to in the text are:

Gather, Comprehensive (GIA Publications, Inc., 7404 South Mason Avenue, Chicago, Ill. 60638)

Hymns for Today's Church (Hodder and Stoughton, 1982)

Laudate – A Hymn Book for the Liturgy (Decani Music, 30 North Terrace, Mildenhall, Suffolk IP28 7AB, 1999)

New English Hymnal (Canterbury Press Norwich, 1986)

Worship – A Hymnal and Service Book for Roman Catholics (GIA Publications Inc., 7404 South Mason Avenue, Chicago, Ill. 60638)